# A Sense of Dance

## Exploring Your Movement Potential

Constance A. Schrader, MA

University of North Carolina at Asheville

Human Kinetics

**Library of Congress Cataloging-in-Publication Data**

Schrader, Constance A., 1953-
    A sense of dance: exploring your movement potential / Constance
A. Schrader.
       p.     cm.
    Includes index.
    ISBN 0-87322-476-0
    1. Dance.   2. Man--Attitude and movement.   3. Human locomotion.
    4. Dance--Political aspects.    I. Title
GV 1595.S33  1996
792.8--dc20

                                                         95-26221
                                                            CIP

ISBN: 0-87322-476-0

© Bill Arnold: Photo on p. 91
© Richard Babb: Figures 2.4 (bonsai tree) and 11.2 and photos on pp. 18 and 98
© Julianne Boling: Figure 2.2
© Tony Brown/RB Studio: Figure 12.2
© F-Stock/Brian Drake: Figure 1.3 (soccer)
© F-Stock/Greg Lashbrook: Photo on p. 76
© F-Stock/Dave Porter: Figure 8.3
© F-Stock/Kevin Syms: Photo 6.2 (Native American dancer)
© IHSA/Jeff Soucek: Figure 1.3 (basketball)
© Tony Mills: Photo on p. 174
Courtesy of NBA Charlotte Hornets: Photo on p. 40
© N.Y. Yankees 1995: Figure 8.1
© Benjamin Porter: Figures 2.3, 3.1, 8.4, 9.1, and 9.2 and photo on p. 175
© Connie Springer: Figure 4.2
© Kathy Triplett: Figure 11.1
© Jack Vartoogian: Figures 1.2 (Sankai Juko performers), 1.3 (Mikhail Baryshnikov), 2.1, 4.3, 6.2 (concert dance), 8.2, and 12.1 and photos on pp. 69, 75, 120, and 157
© Linda Vartoogian: Figures 1.2 (Hula dancer) and 6.1
© Terry Wild Studio: Figure 2.4 (ballet dancer)
© Stuart Witt: Photo on p. 34
© Richard Younker: Figures 1.1 and 4.1

| | |
|---|---|
| Figure 10.1 Rembrandt | The Metropolitan Museum of Art |
| | Rembrandt, Dutch; 1606-1669 |
| | *Aristotle With a Bust of Homer*, oil on canvas |
| | Purchased with special funds and gifts of friends of the Museum, 1961 |
| Figure 10.2 Picasso | The Art Institute of Chicago |
| | Pablo Picasso, Spanish; 1881-1973 |
| | *Nude With Pitcher*, oil on canvas, summer 1906 |
| | Gift of Mary and Leigh Block |
| Figure 10.3 Pollack | The Metropolitan Museum of Art |
| | Jackson Pollack, American; 1912-1956 |
| | *Autumn Rhythm*, oil on canvas |
| | George A. Hearn Fund, 1957 |

**Acquisitions Editor:** Judy Patterson Wright, PhD; **Developmental Editor:** Larret Galasyn-Wright; **Managing Editor:** Julie Marx Ohnemus; **Editorial Assistant:** Coree Schutter; **Copyeditor:** David Frattini; **Proofreader:** Kathy Bennett; **Indexer:** Julie Brown; **Text Designer and Layout Artist:** Jody Boles; **Typesetter:** Francine Hamerski; **Photo Editor:** Boyd LaFoon; **Cover Designer:** Jack Davis; **Cover Photographer:** © Photo Network/Win Brookhouse; **3-Dimensional Figures:** RoundTable Media, Inc.; **Printer:** Versa Press

Printed in the United States of America    10  9  8  7  6  5  4  3  2  1

**Human Kinetics**
P.O. Box 5076, Champaign, IL 61825-5076
1-800-747-4457

*Canada:* Human Kinetics, Box 24040, Windsor, ON N8Y 4Y9
1-800-465-7301 (in Canada only)

*Europe:* Human Kinetics, P.O. Box IW14, Leeds LS16 6TR, United Kingdom
(44) 1132 781708

*Australia:* Human Kinetics, 2 Ingrid Street, Clapham 5062, South Australia
(08) 371 3755

*New Zealand:* Human Kinetics, P.O. Box 105-231, Auckland 1
(09) 523 3462

# Contents

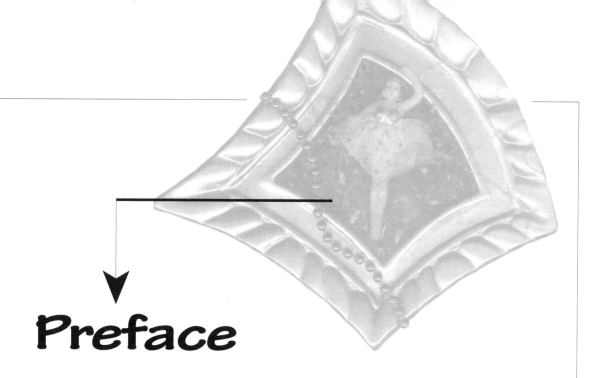

# Preface

**E**very human being has the capacity to create dances that are meaningful, personal, and important. Unfortunately, most people don't feel capable of making dances with any of these qualities. In fact, the longer I teach, the more I discover that people seem to lack confidence in their ability to make *anything* that is meaningful, personal, or important. So this book is not just about making dances. This book is about finding ways to acknowledge who you are and what you know so that you can apply your own unique resources to any creative endeavor.

*A Sense of Dance* is an introduction to dance as creative physical expression. It is written and designed to give you, the beginning dance student, an awareness of and confidence in your movement potential and to help you explore your own resources and talents in observing and reacting to your world using the medium of dance. On another level, this book will awaken you to a new understanding of the historical significance of dance and its pervasive—though not always obvious—influence on our culture.

In *A Sense of Dance*, physical expression is explored from a uniquely personal, internal perspective. This is not to suggest that dance students can learn to dance simply by reading and talking about dance. It *is* to say that you will discover *why* you move and *how* you move and *what* you are most likely to do when you move. In general those answers are your business, and they are part of your development as a dancer, a mover, and an independent thinker. Unlike other dance books, this is not a "How-to" approach but more of a "How-would-you" approach that invites you to discover your own strengths, weaknesses, and preferences and apply that self-awareness to creative expression and observation.

The very qualities that make dance intriguing make dance-making potentially intimidating. As we watch a dance, we participate vicariously with the performer. That is, we compare our physical experience on earth with the movement we see. We are excited and amazed by a performer's ability to become an exceptional human being. We are delighted to be led to discover order revealed in new patterns. We are inspired, stimulated, and awakened when good choreography guides us to a new vision of the world. But when the shoe is on the other foot and *we* are asked to create a dance that will inspire, stimulate, and awaken, where do we begin?

The art of making anything requires inspiration *and* an understanding of the medium in which you are working. For some people the inspiration part comes easily, but they lack the craft to be able to create a unique personal statement. For others the craft part comes easily; that is, they move well and they make nice lines and shapes, but they have a hard time identifying something about the world that interests them as a subject for dance. Finally, there are those who are willing to give movement, and even choreography, a try but who may in fact be quite happy simply becoming educated dance appreciators.

I began the research for this book when I tackled my first composition assignment in graduate school The assignment was to make a dance that dealt with opening and closing. I discovered I had nothing to say; I had no way to begin. There I was, a college graduate with absolutely no idea how to access an original thought. However, a few years later I was living in New York City, dancing and trying to choreograph, although I was still plagued by fears that I had nothing to say. Every movement, idea, and pattern was someone else's. At the height of my frustration I began hitting myself to see if I was as hollow as I felt. It was a lousy feeling. I'm all for healthy self-criticism, but that was ridiculous. And it could have been avoided.

Although I rarely see students physically beating themselves up, I regularly see them in despair—unsure, insecure, and afraid of being thought foolish, clumsy, inappropriate, superficial, or unfit. It's really hard to have a good idea when you question your very core.

I decided to write this book because I think there is room in the world for good ideas, and for new ideas, and I'd like people to start having more of both. I'd like to see the art of dance continue to be a vital part of human culture. I'd like to see dances that reflect fresh perspectives, and I'd like to see people make dances because they are moved by the world. There's power in being able to make sense of the world, in being able to synthesize and translate your experiences into a form that can be shared. Dance is a powerful resource, and getting a *sense* of dance is only the first step in tapping its energy.

Part One

# An Invitation to the Dance

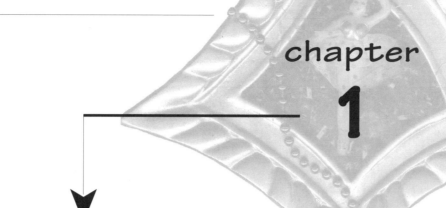

# What Is Dance?

True or False: Dancing is always done to music.

True or False: You need a partner to dance.

True or False: The first ballet dancers were men.

True or False: In order to dance, you need special dance clothes and special training, and it helps if you are thin.

*O*nly one of these statements is true. The first ballet dancers were men. When ballet developed in Europe during the early 1500s, women stood on the sidelines to admire the male dancers' grace and agility. Ballet is just one of numerous dance styles, but because of ballet's cultural dominance, it has almost become synonymous with "dance" in Western cultures.

Every culture has its own dances—rhythmic, stylized ways of using the body to communicate and to celebrate. While music often accompanies dance, it is not always necessary for dancing. As for working with a partner, most—but not all—social dances for entertainment and recreation are done with a partner (Figure 1.1).

**Figure 1.1**
Many social dances are done with a partner, like this Polish folk dance.

The last dance myth—that in order to dance you need special clothes, training, and a thin physique—results from just a few of the misperceptions about dance that Western culture has inherited from hundreds of years of concert dance performed in special costumes, with very specialized training, and by especially thin dancers. These are not conditions for dance participation in the rest of the world. Every culture makes its own rules about what will be considered dance and who may be a dancer. In the past 20 years there have been major changes in our Western orientation to dance. We have had a chance to look at other cultures and to see that expression through movement can be as satisfying to perform as it is to watch (Figure 1.2). Dance is slowly becoming an integral part of Western culture, and you are right on the cutting edge!

**Figure 1.2**
Every culture makes its own rules about what will be considered dance and who may be a dancer. Sankai Juko performers (left) and Hawaiian hula dancers (right) each dance in their own way.

You probably have a few ideas about what dance is. But if you had to explain dance to someone who had not heard of dance, what would you say? How would you describe why people dance? What would you say dance is for? How would you describe what a dancer looks like? Where would you say that dance takes place?

Where are *you* in that description? Do you see yourself as a dancer? Why do you dance, or why do you not dance? How is dance a part of your culture? How is dance a part of your life?

As you dig a little deeper into the world of dance you are likely to confront many of these questions. You may also find yourself thinking in new ways—about what it is to be a moving, responding, communicating creature in your community, in your culture, in your era.

Of course, as you explore dance you won't only be *thinking* in new ways, you will also be *moving* in new ways. Some of these new movements may feel difficult and awkward, while others may feel very easy and natural. Some may appear pointless and others functional, even essential. Other movements may be appropriate to share with your friends, but some will need a special circumstance for performance (on a stage or in a studio). Still other movements will either relax or exhilarate you.

Your study of dance will challenge your ideas about dance. Because you will learn about dance primarily by moving, your study will also challenge some of the ideas you have about yourself—your body image, your creative potential, your coordination. Reading and talking about dance should help you put some of these physical ideas into perspective.

> Part of learning dance is being open to learning new movement patterns—new ways of doing things. Often you will find that your habitual way of moving is only that—a habit—and, if you are willing to explore new ways, you will expand your physical options. For example, cross your arms in front of your chest. Look down, and note which arm is on top. Now uncross your arms, and recross them with the other arm on top. Awkward? Probably, but if you think about it, neither way is right or wrong. You just tried a new movement.

## You Are Always Moving

Freeze. Try not to move anything but your eyes as you read this paragraph. What shape is your body making right now? Are you curled up? Are you stretched out? Are you sitting at a desk, or are you lying on a sofa? Do not move! What body parts are touching? How is your head supported? Does it rest on one hand or on a pillow, or is it balanced on top of your spine? Were you aware of your breathing while you were reading? Now move. Change your posture. Change your position. Change the way you hold yourself. Change your breath.

We are, in fact, always moving. We constantly change our posture to rest different muscles. It is possible to appear to be still, but even when we are not moving our bodies through space, we still move. Try this experiment:

Arrange yourself in a comfortable position where you can see a clock or a watch without changing your position. Your eyes may be open or closed. Now hold this exact, comfortable position for 2 minutes. Try to be completely still.

Even while you were absolutely still for 2 minutes, your chest probably moved as you breathed. Was your belly moving too? What tensions did you discover in your body as you were holding position? How did you relieve those tensions at the end of the experiment? Chances are you moved!

You are always moving, always shifting, always balancing the opposing forces, demands, and desires in your life. Your continuous struggle against the pull of gravity keeps you moving. Sometimes the choices in this struggle are conscious; other times they are unconscious.

Movement as simple as walking involves mastering your relationship with gravity. What does that relationship have to do with dancing? Everything! When you reveal the forces acting on the body, you communicate something about the nature of the moving creature—in this case, you. In the experiment to the left, you could easily use the simple sequence of falling and catching movements for a dance called "Try, try again." By allowing yourself to begin falling, you show yourself succumbing to outside forces; when you catch your weight, the audience will see that you had willfully regained control of your body by opposing the earlier forces. Can you think of other subjects related to losing and regaining control that could be developed simply by working with gravity?

Try this experiment: Stand upright, feet slightly spread. Drop down to your hands and knees, and return to your starting position.

No big deal, right? Now try this experiment: Kneel on the floor, and place this text in front of your knees. Now support your weight on your hands and knees. Exhale, and let your head hang. Very slowly shift the weight to your hands and one knee so that you can bring the other foot up to your hands in preparation for standing. Do you feel the pull of gravity? Did you sense how you had to rebalance or recenter your weight to accomplish this? Freeze in this position long enough to be aware of the balance of tensions required to hold this position.

Here are a few more experiments that explore the simple ways we respond to gravity: Stand with both feet together, arms by your side. Without bending your knees or bending at the waist, see how far forward you can lean before you have to move your feet to catch yourself from falling. Do this a few times to feel the pull of gravity and to find the muscles that have to work harder the farther forward you lean.

What happens when you move your feet apart?

What happens when you bend at the waist?

## Tension and Release

When we move, we change the tension patterns in our bodies. Tension is not necessarily a bad thing. If we had no tension in our bodies, we would not be able to stand up, walk, or run. Without muscle tension, we would not be able to move.

Tension has acquired many negative connotations, especially when used in such contexts as "tension in the Middle East" (preparing to fight), "lower back tension" (pain), and "tension in a relationship" (trouble). But if we look up the etymology of tension, we find that our English word comes from the Old Latin *tanz*, meaning "to stretch." Tanz. Dance. Sound similar? Although there is debate about the origin of the English "dance," many scholars believe that in the history of our language develop-ment, to "stretch" meant to "tense," and "tense" evolved into "dance."

When you dance you tense and stretch to show forces acting on your body. Think about social dancing. What kinds of forces that are acting on your body do you wish to show? Do you want to look as if you are out of control? Do you want to look strong and tough? Do you want to look fluid and sensual? Remember, the forces we are referring to can be physical, emotional, social, or spiri-tual. As you explore creative move-ment or formal dance classes, remember that the way you use ten-sion and stretch will reveal the forces acting on your body.

Imagine how it would feel if you allowed your head to fall forward and then brought it back up to a vertical position. If you were to prac-tice this movement a few more times—letting your head fall far-ther and farther and letting yourself bend more and more each time—you might, finally, let your head fall forward so that the weight took you all the way to the floor.

> Try this experiment: Take two large rubber bands and stretch them between your right and left index fingers so that one band is close to your knuckles and the other band is close to your nails. Get the tension even between the two bands, then stretch the top one even more by bringing your wrists together. What happens to the bottom band? Does it get shorter or longer? The same kind of thing happens in your body as your muscles are engaged in movement. The muscles on one side of a joint tense and become shorter while the muscles on the other side relax to stretch.

If you were to experiment with that progressive shift in weight you would probably not end up in a heap on the floor, right? Why not? Because you would have pro-gressively balanced the tension in your body to avoid injury. Even in the final drop to the floor, you would most likely balance your weight and your speed to control the descent. We control our movements through a balance of tension and relaxation, a combination of resistance and reception.

We are continually balancing the physical, emotional, social, and spiritual forces in our lives. We breathe in, we breathe out. We are happy, we are sad. We work, we rest.

We hope and are sometimes hopeless. We become tense, and we release. In dance, some of these opposites are described as the following contrasts:

Contract—Release          Bound—Loose
Fall—Rebound              Tense—Relax

You know these muscular opposites from your own experience. How about the way your chest and neck muscles feel just before you look at a grade on a test you might have completed well (but then again . . .)? It is a good grade! Contract—Release. How about walking down the street? If you did not rebound after each step, you would have to pick yourself up off the sidewalk between steps. Your weight falls and rebounds; you walk. How about your body's physical change when an authority figure leaves a room? Bound—Loose.

Neither state is better than the other; the balance makes for grace. If we went through life with all muscles contracted, we would move like the Tin Man in *The Wizard of Oz*. Then again, if all our muscles were released all the time, we would not even walk as well as the Tin Man's friend, the Scarecrow. At any time, some of our muscles tense or work while others release or relax. In fact, as our coordination improves with age, muscle groups are trained to contract and to release so that we accomplish tasks without even thinking.

Most of the time, your muscles work in harmony by making adjustments to maintain balance and comfort. Sometimes these adjustments are automatic, other times they are intentional. Surely you remember a time when you had to keep from yawning or slouching because it just was not a good time to show how bored you were? And, surely, you have also caught yourself in the middle of a yawn or a slouch and realized, "Oops! Better straighten up!" Yawns, slouches, sighs, crossed legs, toe-tapping, and pacing are all examples of the personal mannerisms we use to help balance the many forces we face every day. Every day you balance your muscles' tension and release to control and to initiate movement. When you order these natural, physical, human responses, or when you use them for expression and communication, you are, in essence, dancing.

For example: Stand on two feet and place your right hand gently on your right thigh. Slowly raise your right knee to about 45 degrees. As you do this, can you feel the muscle—the quadriceps—tighten? Check the muscles in the back of your leg—the gluteals. Because they are not used to lift the leg, they should be loose. Now see what kind of muscle action occurs if you extend your lower leg. Finally, release all the muscles in the extended leg, let it drop, and notice how the muscles in the other leg have been working.

## You Call This Dance?

The key word here is "order." Any art, good or bad, is the conscious product of a person's effort to create order using a suitable medium. To repeat: When you order natural, physical, human responses, or when you use them for expression, you are dancing. Simply slumping in your chair is not, in and of itself, a dance or an artistic endeavor; however, if and when you deliberately use that movement pattern for effect then you are dancing. Reflexively tapping your toes and drumming your fingers on a desk are not artistic endeavors; these are the body's simple tension-release mechanisms. However, when you order these simple movements to create rhythmic patterns or to call attention to your personal tension by consciously repeating a tapping motion, you are dancing.

You have the skills and the facilities *right now* to consider yourself a dancer. Stretching, tensing, releasing, and all the subtle and not-so-subtle methods we use to balance the forces acting on our bodies are the source materials you need to begin using your body as an instrument of expression. With study comes refinement. But that is no reason to deny the value of your personal movement vocabulary as a starting point.

Let us assume you play soccer. Think about all the soccer movements that involve stretching, tensing, and releasing—all the ways that you balance the forces acting on your body. You have the forces of gravity to deal with when you time your jump for a header; you have the forces of momentum to account for when your opponent intercepts a pass and you need to change direction; you have to stretch your leg as you go for that corner kick; you experience a complete release and recharge when a goal is made, not to mention all the tension patterns that come with running, kicking, throwing, and resting.

You call this dancing? No. We call this soccer, but the soccer movements could be ordered in such a way to communicate something of your personal perspective about the world. Take three of the movements just described: the header, the direction change, and the resting pose. Imagine what could be communicated by ordering these activities as follows:

**Header to right then left; three runs forward; quick stop; three runs backward; hands on knees to resting pose; repeat sequence.**

Can you picture this sequence performed on a stage? Imagine that the dancer goes on using just those three movement patterns in a variety of sequences. Would you imagine a person dealing with physical, emotional, social, or spiritual forces? What might such a dance communicate to you (Figure 1.3)?

## To Dance Is Phenomenal

The art of dance continuously evolves. What was considered dance 100 years ago is different from today's conception. It would be lovely and tidy if we could just define dance and move on, but the art form fairly defies definition. It is better, instead, to accept that because dance evolves to reflect the culture it serves, it is an ever-changing phenomenon. Today, dance serves a wide population base—from the very young to the very old, from the highly trained to the technically untrained dancer—and there is as much controversy as there has ever been about what is, and what is not, dance.

*consider yourself a dancer*

### Figure 1.3

Athletic leaps are not confined to sporting events. How does a leap by Mikhail Baryshnikov communicate a different perspective than a similar movement by a soccer or basketball player?

According to Judith Lynne Hanna, author of *To Dance Is Human*, there are four components that distinguish dance from nondance activities.

1. Dances have a purpose.
2. Dances have intentional rhythm.
3. Dances contain culturally patterned sequences.
4. Dances have extraordinary nonverbal movement which has value in and of itself. (p. 19)

It is true that the purpose of chasing a soccer ball down a field is to put the ball into the opposing team's net. However, this activity, beautiful as it can be, is not played with an intentional rhythm, nor are the physical acts anything other than functional. We would not refer to playing soccer as dancing. While it is also true that digging a ditch has a purpose—to create a place for a new waterway—this activity does not have extraordinary nonverbal movement which has value and beauty in and of itself. We would not refer to digging a ditch as dancing, either.

Yet, if you take a soccer player off the field and have her perform the dribbling and shooting movements on a stage, she would be dancing because the act of framing her movements out of context calls attention to their being extraordinary. Likewise, put the ditchdigger on stage, and you have asked the audience to see something new in his activity. You could also abstract the ditchdigger's movements to create extraordinary nonverbal patterns.

## Why Study Dance?

One of the biggest problems beginning dance students have is believing that they have the capacity to be phenomenal. People who are new to dance often feel that their size, shape, age, gender, and even race make them unsuitable to be real dancers. By this point, it should be clear that dance is an art form in which anyone can participate, contribute, and enjoy. Dance is a phenomenon, and anyone can be phenomenal!

What makes dance an art rather than a sport or a coincidence is the fact that dance is a deliberate activity that involves purpose, intentional rhythm, culturally patterned sequences, and extraordinary nonverbal movement of aesthetic and inherent value. When studying dance you will explore each of those components, and, in doing so, you will learn something about your phenomenal self.

Through your study of dance you will discover three aspects of your phenomenal self: the dancer, the choreographer, and the viewer. In your dance training you will find out more about your body's limits and capabilities. You will explore not only physical but also social, emotional, and spiritual aspects of yourself. In your efforts to apply all that you know to the work you do as a choreographer, you will discover a curiosity for sights, sounds, patterns, and textures. You will learn about yourself as you try new things and experience what you consider to be failures, successes, and the risks of venturing into unfamiliar territory. You will become more aware of your creative voice as you learn about the craft of making dances. You will explore a complex idea and discover its innate simplicity. You will explore a simple idea and discover its innate complexity. As a choreographer you will experience the joy of bringing an original idea into the world.

As a member of a class you will be asked to observe other students on a regular basis. In fact, you will come to rely on the collective wisdom that develops when groups of individual dancers move together. You will learn to observe rather than judge. You will get in touch with a generosity of spirit that comes from working with other classmates and supporting their efforts to discover what works for them. How to be a good collaborator, how to give positive feedback, how to provide constructive criticism, and other skills have value far beyond the classroom and the theater. Learning to appreciate dance will bring you to a new awareness of your self.

The motivation to move is a natural, instinctive response to all the forces which act on our bodies. We are always moving. In order to resist the pull of gravity and move about on the earth, your muscles must work to keep you in an upright position. Even when holding a still shape, you are moving—the muscles that keep your heart pumping and keep you breathing do not stop their pattern of tension and release. Movement is a measure of life, but movement is not necessarily dance. Dance is an art that uses nonverbal movement in an extraordinary way to create a form, order, or statement. Dance reveals the physical, emotional, and social forces that act on a body in such a way to reveal a sense of those forces either for personal benefit or the benefit of an audience. To study dance is to study our phenomenal nature and to explore the personal dimensions of physical, social, and emotional strength, generosity, and wisdom.

Freeze. Relax. Shift. Inhale. Hold your breath. Sigh.
Repeat with more force.
Repeat slowly.
Repeat with dignity.

## Think About It

1. What is your definition of dance? Write down your definition. Underneath yours, write down the definition you find in a dictionary. Then ask three other people for their definitions. What is common to all five answers? How are they different? Create a revised definition now that you have thought more about this concept.

2. If someone had been watching you as you read through this chapter, what could that person have learned about you?

3. For the next 8 hours make a list of the gestures you use. Pay attention to facial gestures, hand gestures, and arm gestures. When you repeat a gesture, such as scratching your nose or biting your nails, put a mark on your list. This may be easier to do with a friend who keeps a list of your gestures while you observe your friend's gesture patterns. How could you form your observations into a dance?

4. Pick a time when it is practical for you to be silent for at least 1 hour. It would be best if you were not by yourself but were, in fact, with other people. Observe how you communicate with them when you are not using words.

5. The next time you are required to wait—for a bus, for a table, for a cashier—observe the way you shift your weight while waiting. How often do you stand with your whole body evenly centered on both feet? Why do so few people stand up straight?

6. Make note of how people you see stand, walk, and gesture. Try some of these patterns on your own body.

7. Observe a moving animal, a moving, rooted object (like a tree or a flower), and a moving human. Consider how all movement reflects change, and discuss the changes evident in the movements you observe.

# How Do You Learn to Dance?

A woman was preparing a report on folk dancing. While doing her research she met an 88-year-old man who had been clogging (an American folk dance) all his life. Thrilled to have found such an authority, she asked him to show her some of his steps. He danced for her, and she was very impressed. "That one with the swipe," she asked, "would you please show me that one again?" She tried to duplicate the man's pattern. "Excuse me," she interrupted, "is that shuffle-step or shuffle-hop?" He started over, a little slower, and again she interrupted, "Is it a flap or another shuffle before the scuff?" Sighing, the polite man started over, and again the eager scholar stopped his dance. "Oh, I see!" she said, "but do you change your weight on the 2 or the 3?" The man stopped again and simply asked, "Darlin', do you want to dance or do you want to talk about it?"

## Learning About Dance and Learning to Dance

You signed up for a dance course because you wanted to move, but now you may be frustrated because the course requires you to read. You may, however, be a research-oriented person who prefers to gather information before beginning, or you might just be confused about what reading has to do with dancing.

Both learning about dance and learning to dance can be approached from several angles. It is possible to learn dance steps from a single teacher without researching other styles or reading other background information about dance. It is possible to choreograph dances without studying the principles of composition. Chances are, the veteran clog dancer learned his dance style, not by reading about it or by asking a bunch of technical questions, but by imitating and experimenting with what he saw. This is the *dive-right-in* approach to learning about dance and learning to dance. Others include the *creative-movement* and the *technical* approaches.

Using an analogy to clarify these three methods, let us say that you are interested in working with wood. You would use the dive-right-in approach if you decided that the best way to learn about woodworking was to hang around the shops of some woodworkers and to see what tips and skills you could pick up. By watching them, talking with them, and helping them with their projects, you would eventually get the hang of woodworking and feel confident about starting your own projects. The creative movement approach would include collecting pictures of woodworking designs that interested you and, possibly, checking out an instructional book from the library. You would read about different kinds of wood, joints, and tools, collect some materials, and play with what you have in order to see what you can make. The technical approach would land you in a class taught by a master woodworker who would lead you through a series of skills and give you constant feedback to correct your developing skills. If you wanted to build a house, you would probably draw a little bit from all three of these approaches. Each has its merits and appropriate applications, but each also has its pitfalls.

## The Dive-Right-In Approach

The dive-right-in approach is usually the one used to pass down folk dances, including the dances you and your friends do. There are studios that teach social dances, such as the jitterbug, the mambo, or the fox-trot, but contemporary dances are learned by doing. No reading, no writing, and no special classes. You go to a dance, and you dive right in. You normally find this approach used in dances that have limited movement vocabularies, or a limited selection of basic steps. Clog dancing, for instance, is based on eight basic steps that the dancers modify according to their individual styles. Clogging is done more for recreational and social purposes than for concert performance. Although there are clogging teams and competitions, clogging is, in general, a social dance that encourages and celebrates individual stylistic differences. In fact, these inventions keep the dance alive with fresh innovation. As with other popular social dances, one movement pattern (usually very repetitive) will be slightly varied (either by intention or by accident), giving birth to a new pattern. The dance will evolve as others try out this new movement and, invariably, add their own flair to the pattern.

If you have access to a TV that gets MTV, compare dance videos by noting what makes one artist's dance style the same or different from other artists' styles. Notice in particular what kinds of patterns are repeated to create a style. If you attend social dances, look for repeating movement patterns among your peers on the dance floor.

On the other hand, many folk and other ritualized dances are valued for their celebration of tradition. It's the performer's responsibility to honor that tradition by repeating the dance in a form that resembles the original as much as possible; therefore, many dances of this type are not a good outlet for choreographic creativity. However, traditional dances have long been a source of material and inspiration for choreographers who have adapted traditional patterns to fit their own work.

## The Creative Movement Approach

The creative movement approach celebrates spontaneity, originality, and individuality through structured movement opportunities in which the dancer continuously invents movement according to personal preferences. Most of the time this opportunity is not a free-for-all; it is structured to encourage personal investigation into some particular aspect of movement. The creative movement approach is an incredibly useful way to learn about your personal movement preferences, analyze your strengths and weaknesses, and explore new territory. That new territory may be physical, social, emotional, or a combination of all three.

To the right is an example of a creative movement exercise. Which of the steps do you think would be the most challenging? Or, to put the question another way, in which of the steps could you most challenge yourself? Would those explorations present you with a physical challenge? Would you feel awkard or uncomfortable making those explorations in the presence of others? Would you be afraid of putting yourself in that exploring frame of mind no matter who was watching? Would you be afraid that you were doing the exploration in the wrong way? These physical, social, and emotional challenges are the very reasons that some dancers are attracted to the resources of the creative movement approach to dance. It assumes no previous dance training, it encourages innovation, and it is an approach which honors the

In a creative movement class you might be asked to do an exercise like this: Pick a simple gesture. (A gesture is a movement pattern that has social significance, such as waving your hand, scratching your head, or dropping your face into your hands.) Repeat your gesture a few times to get the sense of its rhythm and its muscularity. (For now, let us use a shrug of the shoulders.)

Now repeat your gesture ten times, varying the speed of the gesture and moving extraordinarily quickly and extraordinarily slowly.

Now explore the same kind of action as your original gesture with another part of your body. (Shrug your hips; shrug your knees.)

Now explore the same kind of action as your original gesture but pretend that the gesture is leading you through the room. (For example, a shrug of the shoulders takes you backward, forward, sideways, into the air, or down to the ground.)

experience and resources of individuals at whatever stage they arrive. However, dancers must be careful not to get too comfortable with one mode of creating and moving—if this familiarity continues, everything a dancer creates will be very similar. Instead, dancers interested in this approach should continue to find challenging structures and push themselves to generate new solutions and refine their movements.

## The Technical Approach

Traditionally, learning about dance and learning to dance required you to be a copycat. We call this the technical approach because you copy a dance technique that has been identified and valued as worthwhile for training. This technical approach to learning dance celebrates the history and traditions of time-honored training methods; it is devoted, not to inventing new movements, but to accurately repeating a syllabus of movements that has been recognized as a style distinct from other methods (Figure 2.1). It is the student's duty to master the nuances of movement necessary to continue the historical tradition. You achieve this goal by rigorously repeating specific movement patterns for hours and by practicing those patterns as strictly physical skills.

Although a teacher might offer an image to help a student or class understand a movement pattern, it is still up to the students to repeat the patterns as closely as possible to the way they have been demonstrated. For instance, a teacher might suggest that the students imagine a soft breeze lifting the arms, but it would not be appropriate in a ballet class for students to let their arms float up wherever their imaginations dictate. No student could sustain interest in such repetition without maintaining a curiosity about the possible nuances of the exercises; the students need to sustain a commitment to increasing their skills and range of motion, as well as to recognizing and executing the given patterns.

**Figure 2.1**

By imitating the forms demonstrated by the t'ai chi master, the student discovers a rhythm of breath and weight and a grace that comes from their integration.

In many situations some aspects of the dive-right-in, creative movement, and technical approaches will add variety to the learning process. As you work, bear in mind that whatever style you are interested in pursuing, the dance has a tradition and a history. Even the newest dance craze has its roots in some moment in the history of dance. Reading and talking about that history are valuable to a complete understanding of the art form, but the most critical source of knowledge will come from moving, doing, and dancing. Regardless of which approach you choose, the beginning dancer will work with five fundamental movement experiences.

# Fundamental Movement Experiences

Whether you want to learn a tour jeté or a time step, whether you want to break old habits, learn old patterns, or create new ones, your job is to integrate these five fundamental movement experiences as you work: analyzing the actions of the spine, determining locomotor versus axial motion, working with rhythmic coordination, moving with functional alignment, and moving from your center.

## Actions of the Spine

The spine can perform three actions: It can bend, twist, or extend. Your spine is composed of 26 vertebrae, and any of the three actions is possible at each of the joints. Pretty amazing potential! Remember that the three actions can be useful in two ways. First, as a strategy for copying other people's movements, begin by recognizing the actions of the spine. Is the spine vertical? Is only the lumbar spine (the lowest third) vertical and the rest bent? Is the spine bent and twisted? When trying to read movement, look for what the action of the spine might be.

Explore the potential of your spine to bend by lying on your back and slowly bringing yourself up to a curled, sitting position. Roll back down to your back by trying to let each vertebra touch the ground, one at a time. Imagine what your spine would look like if the room were dark and only your spine glowed in the dark. What other ways can you bend your spine? You have done forward flexion and back flexion. How about side flexion?

In a sitting position, twist your head as far as you can without moving your shoulders. You are twisting your cervical spine. Now, without moving your pelvis, continue to twist, allowing the action to travel down through your thoracic spine. Let your hips move, allowing the twist to also occur in your lumbar spine. Rewind, keeping your head as twisted as possible.

Have you ever played with one of those toys that collapse when you push the bottom and then stand up again when you let the button go? If you have seen one, you remember that the little creature is held together with rubber bands that stretch when you press and go taut again when you release the button. Using that same image, slump over so your spine is bent and twisted. Now bring your spine back to vertical. You just extended your spine.

Secondly, apply the bend, twist, and extend motions to your creative efforts. If you want to make your movement patterns more visually interesting, try changing the shape of your spine as you move. Use these actions as a condition of movement, that is, work with a continuously bent or twisted shape. In a technique class you will find that your spine determines the basic shape of your movement and establishes the particular relationship to gravity that the technique honors. Ballet, for instance, displays a freedom from the force of gravity, so the spine is generally vertical. Jazz dance, which often deals with the contrasts of power and submission, uses the spine to indicate those two conditions. Modern dance makes shapes that may or may not pertain to the force of gravity. This may be one of the reasons people find some modern dances inherently confusing—their intuition tells them one thing, and the dance says something else! As a dancer and a dance appreciator, you can use this information to clarify your intentions and those of a choreographer.

The audience will perceive the line of force acting on a body as perpendicular to the line of the spine. Therefore, a spine which is vertical will create an image of balance or freedom from strain against gravity. A bent spine will create an image of a weakened or submissive form. A twisted spine will create an image of mutually opposing forces.

## Locomotor Versus Axial Movement

Another fundamental movement experience distinguishes between moving through space and moving in place. In dance, when we say "moving through space," we are not talking about rockets; we are referring to the volume of the dance area in which the dancer works. This space could be a classroom, the stage area, or even a parking lot or field. Dancers have two options when it comes to moving: They can move through space by walking, running, leaping, or skipping, or they can move on a spot. Actions which take the body through space are called *locomotor* movements. Actions which do not take the body through space are *axial* movements. This distinction serves two purposes; you can use it to read dance more effectively, and you can use it as a tool for improvisation.

## Rhythmic Coordination

Athletes are aware of the importance of rhythmic coordination, and they use rhythm in their training. Rhythmic coordination helps a basketball player achieve elevation and timing for a lay-up. The rhythm of the step-step-jump pattern has been practiced repeatedly and helps to time when to shoot the basket. Competitive swimmers use the rhythmic coordination of their stroke patterns to pace themselves and to sense their speed. The use of rhythmic patterns in motor activities—from competitive sports to vacuuming a rug—enables the participant to settle into a groove, put the body on automatic pilot, and free the mind for decisions, such as when to shoot or pass. In dance, as in the martial arts, we seek this freedom for its own sake, as an end in itself. There is a difference between the application of rhythmic coordination in dance and its use in sports; the rhythm is intentional in dance while it is functional in sports (Figure 2.2).

To explore the distinction between locomotor movement and axial movement, try this experiment (you will need a fairly open space in which to work): Imagine there is an X on the floor, and you have your hands and feet on each of the four points of that X. With your pelvis off the center of the X, and your hands and feet glued to their spots, move as much as possible as you count to four. Then, cover as much space as possible as you count to four, moving anywhere except on the X. When you get to four counts, freeze with two feet and one hand glued to the floor. Again, move as much as possible as you count to four, then move anywhere else (running, leaping, rolling) as you count to four, this time ending on one foot. By bending, twisting, and extending, move on this new spot for a count of four, then move anywhere else as you count to four, ending on your bottom for one, final count of four during which you move however you can. Conclude by making a still shape. Anything you did while you were not on an X was a locomotor movement. Everything you did with one or more points fixed to the ground was axial movement.

*rhythm is intentional in dance while it is functional in sports*

**Figure 2.2**

Similar movements can have very different rhythmic functions.

Rhythmic coordination is a fundamental movement experience that will be explored in any of the three approaches to learning dance. Intentional rhythm distinguishes dance from other movement activities. As you learn to dance or as you learn about dance, you will become aware of the importance of rhythmic coordination. Rhythmic coordination can mean moving to the music, but let us not limit ourselves to working with music. Sometimes dance is performed in silence, to a text, or to music that has no recurring pattern of beats. Likewise, in many dance activities, rhythmic coordination, through its predictability and its familiarity, invites an ease of movement and a freedom of mind.

## Functional Alignment

If you needed to dig a ditch, you would not hold your shovel with both hands on the end. Depending on what you needed to dig up, you would move your hands closer to or farther from the head for maximum leverage. Becoming aware of functional alignment in dance is a bit like learning to choke up on a shovel. The more you work and the more you come to understand your personal strengths and weaknesses, the more you will discover how important it is to work in the most balanced, relaxed manner. You are constantly balancing the forces of nature, resisting the pull of gravity, and responding to millions of muscular changes in the course of the day (Figure 2.3). When you begin forming your dance movement, you need to be conscious of working so that your joints are protected and that your strength and flexibility are most easily accessed.

**Figure 2.3**
Our position changes in response to natural forces as well as the task at hand.

## Moving From Your Center

Moving from your center is probably the most elusive of all the five fundamental movement experiences. The concept of center is an intriguing one. Anyone who has cornered on a motorcycle or ridden a surfboard will tell you that your center is not a specific X-marks-the-spot place on the body. In the same way, a dancer's center is not a spot you can put an X on, nor is it a place you can feel with your hands. When you dance, your center is your physical, emotional, and spiritual source of strength and balance. Martial arts rely on this sense of center for power, speed, and effective movement. It is not a power that comes with bulky muscles; it is a power that comes with grace, agility, and a cultivated ability to chose the right movement option at the right moment. Moving from your center is the ability to be completely invested in your movement.

Here is a concrete example: The teacher asks the class to imagine and to explore the experience of being surrounded by flies. The dancer who is not working from her center will be the one standing in a corner half-heartedly waving her arms while looking around to see if anyone else is watching her. The dancer who is working from his center will be the one turning, ducking, swiping, going to the floor, and running from the spot he started on. One person attempts the motion of swatting but is too nervous about what other people think to become emotionally motivated by the image of flies. The other person is completely invested in manifesting the movement physically, emotionally, and spiritually.

move from your center

Take another example. The teacher asks the class to make an interesting dance presentation using the following sequence: Take two steps forward, one step back to turn, and spiral to the floor. The dancer moving from her center will create a reason for being drawn forward, then back, then to the floor. She will explore different feelings of force that could be responsible for such a sequence. Pushing, pulling, balancing, and tensing will be part of her explorations. She will allow herself to have an experience and will therein discover a compelling, personal investment in the sequence.

The person who is not moving from his center will be more mental, checking the mirror (if there is one in the room) to see how he looks, probably trying to move according to some idea about how a dancer should look. He will be looking around at others who are working, not trying to pick up ideas but self-consciously checking to see if anyone is watching him. This caution is entirely normal, especially among beginning students. Unfortunately, it is not a productive work habit, and it generally results in inhibiting access to the magic that waits to be discovered in each individual.

Learning to move from your center means learning to trust your own resources. As these centered moments come to you, you will realize that moving from your center is not only a fundamental movement experience, it is a fundamental life experience.

The five fundamental movement experiences are important for a beginning dancer but are equally important to a more advanced dancer learning to take new risks and pushing to new levels of dance mastery.

## What Does It Mean?

Perhaps you sympathize with the girl standing in the corner half-heartedly swatting but not willing to get any more involved. It might be that you have been asked to practice an exercise that does not seem to have any purpose other than pain and frustration. You may find yourself thinking, "Sure, I could do that, but what does it mean?"

### The Purpose of Dance

In a Nigerian village the women perform a special dance as they lay a floor in a new hut, but it would not be accurate to say that the purpose of the dance is to lay a floor. The purpose of the dance is to make the floor-laying a magical experience. When the young girls of a European village are collected to skip around a maypole holding ribbons, they do eventually cover the pole in bright colors, but that is not the purpose of the dance. The maypole dance celebrates spring. In our increasingly utilitarian culture, many new to dance wonder what purpose dance serves.

The purpose of dance will vary for different people. Those who enjoy social dance probably find that they like being with other people; they enjoy moving with other people, and they like the way they feel after dancing. Those who enjoy taking creative movement classes want to use their imaginations and learn about themselves by solving problems using their bodies. Those who are attracted to formal dance classes appreciate the rewards of rigorous training as they discover more physical potential.

Among those who create (choreograph) dances, there are different ideas about the purpose of presenting their efforts to others. Some wish to share the thrill and joy of moving. Some hope that the movement patterns they have put together will be so impressive to a viewer that simply to watch will be an exhilarating experience. Other choreographers deliberately avoid the use of highly trained movement, hoping instead to establish fellowship with their audience by using a vocabulary that is within the average person's capability. There are choreographers who are interested in exploring an aspect of the human physical potential and in presenting the fruits of these explorations. There are also those whose work draws on each of these agendas.

## Finding Meaning in Your Own Dancing

Your purpose for dancing will be personal. The meaning you get from watching a dance or from dancing will be a personal response. As you study, you will find memories, emotions, and ideas being triggered. You will find that your capacity to sense the world will become more acute; you will see more, hear more, feel more, and generally be more alive to your world.

Learning to observe the movement (and stillness!) in the world is a lifelong practice—the more you know, the more you see. Learning to read movement is an important skill, not only in your dance class, but in other aspects of your life. It is your job, as a student of movement, to collect interesting patterns, postures, gestures, and movements from nature, friends, strangers, animals, and every aspect of your experience. It is your job to discover what fascinates *you* about the moving world.

As you begin to apply that fascination to create dances, even short dance studies will require that you develop your capacity to hone your ideas and to make a gift of those ideas to others. You will find both the frustration and the satisfaction of trying to create order out of what could be a chaos of ideas. Developing your creative capacities will be beneficial in many areas of your life beyond the dance studio or auditorium.

## Training, Exploring, and Forming Your Own Style

Regardless of your approach to dance—dive-right-in, creative movement, technical, or some combination of these approaches—your efforts to become proficient will involve three processes: training, exploring, and forming. And as you integrate these processes, you will be developing a *style*.

## Style

Dance is a word that describes an enormous range of movement activities which are grouped and categorized by many different titles. There is a broad category called folk dance, in which you find dances such as the electric slide, hula, schottische, Morris, and hat dance. There is

*develop a style*

the more narrow category of ballet, in which you find techniques such as the Cecchetti, Royal Academy, and Vaganova. Modern dance boasts almost as many techniques as dancers. In this category you find big names such as Graham, Cunningham, Limón, and Horton. Some differentiate among these, referring to different techniques as a distinct style of dance. This is accurate to the extent that each of these techniques is characteristic of an individual, period, school, or custom. But for the sake of this book, we will use style to refer to an individual's manner of movement, assuming that each person's manner is a unique compilation of personal experience and expertise.

Every moving person has a style of dance. Trained or untrained, we all have a personal signature to the way we dance. Granted, many people claim that they do not dance, but if even these people were willing to relinquish their inhibitions long enough to share a tiny bit of their dancing spirits, you would see that they, too, have a dance style.

Close your eyes and picture a dancer. What image came to mind? What was this dancer wearing? Was this dancer still or moving?

Now close your eyes and picture yourself dancing. In what ways are these two images similar? In what ways are they different? How much of your dance style is an imitation of dancers you have seen, and how much is your own?

Finally, close your eyes and picture one of your parents dancing.

Three different people. Did you imagine three different dance styles? Three different ways of moving and expressing? If you drew a blank on any of these images, why do you think that might be?

Style comes from your soul as well as your body. You can train your body to execute movements and patterns, but the way those are actually performed reflects the physical, emotional, social, and spiritual aspects of your unique nature.

## Training

Training is important if you want to achieve mastery in a particular skill, but bear in mind all of the skills that are available to pursue through work in dance. Physical, emotional, social, and spiritual growth are all a part of learning to dance as well as learning about dance. Physical training will help you develop your instrument—your body—so that you have the possibility to physically realize a great diversity of movement. Rigorous physical training is not a prerequisite for being able to enjoy dance or to choreograph a dance, but both an awareness and acceptance of your physical limits and strengths are such prerequisites.

Training is nothing more than dedicating thought and attention to some aspect of personal development in order to direct the growth of your skills. You are training if you repeat technical skills, if you try to develop more strength and flexibility, or if you attempt to access a new level of creative potential (Figure 2.4).

*Style comes from your soul as well as your body.*

**Figure 2.4**

External guidance and correction are often essential parts of the training process.

Training might mean paying attention to the way you sit, stand, or run. You are directing the growth of your powers of observation in everyday activities. Training might mean that you deliberately choose to work with a new partner in class. You might wish to use your dance class as a place to direct your social and emotional growth. Training might mean keeping a journal of sights, sounds, smells, thoughts, reactions, feelings, and other food for choreographic thought. Training might also mean something as simple and as spiritual as learning how to fall, how to move backward without looking, or how to share your work with your classmates.

Your dance training will involve observation, not only of your teachers, but also of other classmates. We learn so much from watching other people. But, try as we might, we can never be just like Paula Abdul, MC Hammer, Fred Astaire, Mikhail Baryshnikov, or even the best dancer in the class. You can certainly benefit from their imagination and inspiration, but if you ignore or fail to develop your own creative voice, your dances will lack the very spark you so admire in others. Ultimately, you must be able both to use ideas you have gained from others and to enjoy the uniqueness of your own ideas.

cultivate creativity

## Exploring

A sense of adventure is disappearing from daily experience. It is impossible to avoid advertising, so much of which is geared to sell solutions to problems rather than encourage investigation of how those problems may have occurred in the first place. Much of education is geared either to reiterating the correct answer or to deducing what it is that a teacher wants to hear. Given the present information overload from all the media, it is easy to be seduced into believing that there is nothing new to explore. In fact, nothing could be farther from the truth. The problem is that creative curiosity has temporarily fallen out of fashion. You are in charge of cultivating your creative curiosity. You are responsible for finding magic in who you are and what you do, and dance class is a great place to develop those skills—skills which will also pour into other aspects of your life.

Exploration in dance might mean that, as you repeat a movement pattern, you explore reaching a little farther or rotating a little more. It might mean that you play (yes, play!) with the tension you are working with or the forces that motivate your movement. Exploration might mean that, when given creative flexibility, you see what it is like to move more quickly than you normally would, or more slowly. Exploration might mean that you allow yourself to begin whether or not you are sure you will succeed. Allow yourself to process without worrying about product. It is a bit like playing with a piñata: In order to get to the goodies inside, you have to be willing to swing at the target without being able to see it.

There is a great temptation, especially among beginning dancers, to plan everything rather than to explore or to experiment. All too often, students avoid movement by having discussions and asking questions. How should we begin? Who stands where? What costumes could we wear? How will it end? But what does it mean? They substitute <u>talk</u> for <u>action</u> because they are not sure what is expected and are afraid of doing the assignment incorrectly. And on a more basic level, beginning dancers, like most people, are afraid of looking like fools in front of an audience; they would rather do nothing than do something that risks making them appear inept or inadequate. Understandable. But how do we get around this? Better yet, how might you avoid this pitfall yourself?

## Forming

Forming is part of any artistic pursuit. Following any of the three approaches to learning dance, you will find yourself forming patterns and sequences that have physical, social, emotional, and sometimes spiritual significance for you. Training, exploring, and forming are interconnected aspects of the creative process. While you are training, you explore new ways to form your body into desirable shapes, and you explore new ways to accomplish new goals. When you are exploring, you are training yourself to operate with curiosity and to suspend judgment, and you are forming unique patterns motivated by your personal interests and skills.

When you bring form to your work, whether that work is a 4-count study or a 40-minute piece, you bring your training, and the fruits of your exploration, into concerted focus. For the sake of an audience, for the sake of your classmates, and for the sake of your own satisfaction, forming is the springboard of the art of dance.

In subsequent chapters we will look at how daily life applies to dance, and how the art of dance applies to daily life. We will examine the elements of dance and the differences between dance statements and dance reactions. Finally, we will look at the process of using dance for thoughtful, deliberate self-expression. We will explore perception and creativity in an effort to awaken you to the possibilities of using dance as a valuable, functional way of expressing your humanity.

## Think About It

1. If you enjoy social dancing, think about the kind of dancing you do, and focus on one movement pattern that you feel you do well. How did you learn that pattern? How is the way you perform that different from the way other people do it? (You may have to look very closely, but you will find a difference.) Which of the approaches did you use to learn that pattern? Are you still improving on it? What made you want to learn to dance to begin with?

2. Think about some of the ways in which you utilize rhythmic coordination in your daily life. Name at least three activities. How is it that these activities lend themselves to rhythmic movement? If you were to impose a rhythm on an activity, for instance, brushing your hair, how would that activity change? Would you now call this activity a dance?

3. How can a dance have meaning?

4. If you had to choose, would you rather watch a dancer who could

   a. perform amazing acrobatic feats,
   b. reveal to you a sad or beautiful aspect of being human, or
   c. present intriguing patterns and shapes with no literal or narrative reference?

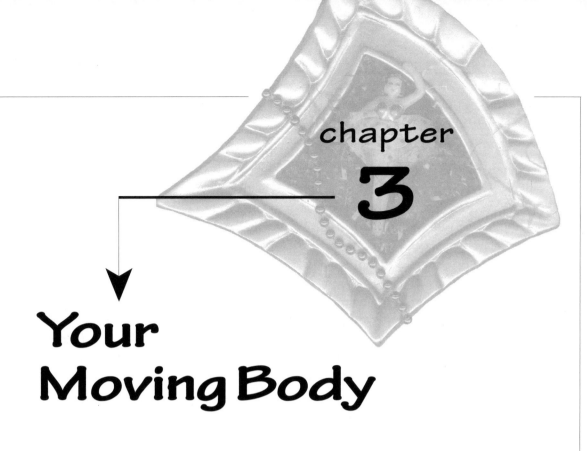

# Your Moving Body

**I**f it seems to you that we keep flipping back and forth between discussing dance as separate from daily life and as part of it, you are exactly right. We have established that there are aspects of dance that separate dance activity from similar physical activities. We have discussed the differences we might expect to find among various kinds of dance, such as social, concert, and creative movement dance. In the next chapter we will look at the elements of dance and the ways that those elements are part of daily activities. When creating or appreciating dance as a performance art, we intuitively apply our experiences with these elements by relating the use of time, space, and effort with our personal experiences.

In this chapter we continue to draw from information that you are familiar with—your own body. In this chapter you will be asked to consider the mechanics of movement, basic movement patterns, and a little basic anatomy so that you will have a better understanding of your movement potential.

Each body is unique. Your ability to imitate another person's movement will be determined not just by your skill in reading movement but also by the physical potential that you have developed by this time in your life. Likewise, your ability to create movement patterns will be determined by what you have either seen or tried in your lifetime. This chapter will help you both to realize how much you already know and to build on that knowledge in a healthy, personal way.

## The Body Is an Instrument

*The moving body is a unique instrument.*

You need a musical instrument in order to make music. Whatever instrument a musician chooses—flute, guitar, synthesizer, violin, harmonica, even the human voice—that musician must become familiar with the instrument if it is to be played with control. It is possible to play any instrument and elicit sound, but in order to make music with skill you need to learn the instrument and practice playing it. Your body is your instrument for dance. We are all able to use our bodies as instruments to express feelings. Studying dance is like practicing an instrument; by sharpening your natural skills and increasing your range and potential through practice, you increase your ability to play your instrument.

Let us begin by investigating the art of moving, starting with movements as simple as walking or bending. These are movement patterns you mastered as a child, patterns which are so familiar you may not even know them by name (Figure 3.1). We will look at movement for the sake of accomplishing a goal or a task and movement done for the sheer pleasure and satisfaction it can bring. We will consider the ways a body might move from one place to another, and the ways a body might move on one spot. Finally, we will consider the moving body as a unique instrument to be explored, played, and celebrated for its unique potential.

The use of the body as an instrument of expression is less respected and encouraged in Western culture than in other cultures, so it is often the case that, beginning in adolescence, people start to feel uncomfortable exploring their physical potential. This is unfortunate because, as we discussed in the first two chapters, the expressive use of the body is a natural part of living. Most children enjoy running, leaping, sliding, spinning, and imitating the ways things move in the real world and in their imaginations. Animals, clouds, kings, queens, bugs, fish, ghosts, armies, and fairies are all found in children's play. They enjoy moving for the sake of moving and creating for the personal mastery it brings. They enjoy sharing their efforts with admiring audiences. To them, moving is magic. It is

**Figure 3.1**

We learn the fundamentals of movement, like leaping and running, as children.

possible to recapture that magic as we explore in a more mature way all the potential we have for using our bodies.

When considering your own movement potential, be aware that there is a temptation, especially among beginners, to be negative—to focus on all the things that feel wrong, awkward, or incompetent. Use the body as an instrument to focus on the kinds of sounds that you make easily and well, then gradually build your repertoire by practicing, experimenting, and refining your physical voice. You can bet that John Coltrane and Miles Davis made one or two squeaks before they mastered their horns. Be willing to observe without judging. Be willing to explore. Leave your mind and body open to discovery through trial and error. The way that you work with your instrument will be your unique gift to the world. That is worth working on.

When you learn an instrument you start out with the fundamentals and build from there, so let us take the same approach. Let us break moving into two categories: *moving in one place* (axial movement) and moving from one place to another (locomotor movement). We will call the second category *moving through space* and start our exploration there.

## Moving Through Space

Space usually means off the planet or outer space, so the idea of moving through space brings images of weightlessness, white oxygen suits, and walks on the moon. Let us look at moving through space in a more earth-centered way. Let us think of space as synonymous with area, volume, or room.

What is the space between you and this book, between you and the nearest window, and between your feet? What is the space from the floor to the ceiling and from the ground to the lowest limb of a tree you can see? When you consider space you are considering not just distance but volume, all the air and the straight or jagged perimeters that define the space in question.

Look at the space between you and the nearest door. Can you name three

Try these experiments and begin to explore the potential of just one body part in space. ▪ Move your hand up, down, toward, and away from the book. ▪ Make your hand float, now dart, now squirm. ▪ Lead with your little finger up to the top left corner, and then use your thumb to lead the hand to the bottom left corner. ▪ Using your left hand, imagine that there is a strong force that you need to overcome as you press your hand to the right. ▪ Now try holding your arm still so that your hand stays in one place in this space between you and the book. What movements can your hand make with your wrist fixed in space? ▪ Open and shut, one digit moving at a time, twisting, curling. When we think of moving through space, it is easy to think of moving in a wide, open space such as a field or a huge room, but you just proved that there are a lot of ways to move through even a very small space!

ways of moving that would take you from your chair to that door? Write down a series of steps, including how many of each one, and in what order these steps should occur. If you are in a feasible space, try your series and find out what it takes to accomplish the whole series in the space available. If not, use your imagination to predict how the sequence you created could be performed. Remember, space equals volume, not distance. Moving through space can involve moving close to the ground, through the air, moving side-to-side, doubling back on your path, pushing, pulling, and so on. Consider moving through space as challenging and interesting as you care to make it. Reconsider the space between you and the door, and imagine all the possible ways that you could work with the three words you chose.

If you included the words run, walk, jump, hop, leap, crawl, or roll to describe your movement through the space to the door, you named one of the seven basic locomotor patterns. Each of these patterns is a different way of moving your body through space. To accomplish any of these locomotor movements, and thus move through space, you need to find a way to get your weight off of one spot and onto another, that is, you need to transfer your weight from one place to another.

Each of these locomotor patterns is a specific way of transferring weight so that the body moves through space. As a child you probably used all of these patterns in your play without even thinking about the distinctions among them. As a dancer you will also use these patterns, but you will probably be more conscious of which pattern is which. When learning patterns in class it is useful to recognize such distinctions. When making creative choices as a choreographer it is useful to recognize one pattern from another so that you can repeat or refine your choices and so that you can work more clearly with other dancers. As dancers, let us take a look at the basic locomotor patterns.

## Basic Locomotor Patterns

A locomotor pattern is a movement pattern which is used to transport the body from one place in space to another.

The first locomotor movement an infant makes is a roll, a transfer of weight from one side to the opposite side which causes the body to flip. Another infant-related movement pattern is crawling, a pattern in which the weight of the body is transferred from one leg and its opposite arm to the other leg and arm. Next comes walking, which, like crawling, involves transferring the weight from one foot to the other while counterbalancing with the opposite arm. A run is related to a walk in that the weight of the body is transferred from one leg to the other, but in a walk the body never completely leaves the ground, while in a run there is a moment of air time—time when the whole body is off the ground. Check this out for yourself. If your weight transfer keeps you in the air even longer, you are leaping. What happens in a hop? Do you transfer your weight to the other leg? What is the difference between a hop and a jump?

Because these locomotor movements are the basic vocabulary of natural, human movements, they are the building blocks of dance. Any dance step which involves moving through space can be described in terms of the basic locomotor patterns. Test

THE BUILDING BLOCKS OF DANCE

this by taking one of your popular social dances and writing down the names of the movements that make up the pattern you recognize. If you can keep this simplicity in mind as you try to imitate dance moves, you will discover that what you are really trying to learn are new ways of combining steps you already know!

## Complex Locomotor Patterns

Looking at locomotor patterns, we find basic patterns combined to form more complex patterns. Some of these patterns are personal patterns, cultural patterns, and patterns found all over the globe. As a student of dance you will find it useful to learn movement sequences by recognizing the locomotor patterns within complex movements. Eventually, you will find that some of the basic patterns are frequently combined in the same order, so, by recognizing these complex patterns, you can simplify your learning.

Take, for instance, a complex pattern called skipping. A skip, which is a combination of a walk and a hop, is a good example of a complex pattern made up of basic locomotor patterns. Because you learned to skip as a child, you no longer see that sequence as a step-hop combination but rather recognize the whole pattern as a skip. When learning a sequence of steps that includes this complex pattern, you simply plug in the skip considered as one pattern instead of two.

In each style of dance you study you will find complex locomotor patterns that move the dancer through space using the same, repeating series of basic locomotor patterns. Some of these patterns have names, and some simply come and go with fashion.

Many of the named patterns describe some special activity or effect that the pattern creates. For instance, a *pas de chat*, a common, complex pattern in ballet, translates to "step of cat." The pattern is a combination of a step and a leap which becomes cat-like

Is it possible to transfer your weight without going anywhere? Sure it is! As we said in chapter 1, we are continuously changing our postures when slumping, standing tall, leaning to one side or another, or crossing and uncrossing our arms and legs. But these transfers of weight do not move through space. If you transfer your weight without moving your feet (or your knees, your side, or whatever body part is supporting you) through space, you will not go anywhere. Get yourself a pen and experiment with this idea of weight transfer by holding your pen in one hand and exploring different ways to get the object to the other hand. Explore ways of making the transfer of weight slowly and gradually. Explore ways of making the transfer quickly. Now look back at your seven basic locomotor patterns, and see if you can identify which weight transfers are similar to the ones we humans use to move through space. What is the difference between a roll and a hop? What is the difference between a walk and a leap? Now, what would you say is the difference between rockin' and rollin'?

Some complex patterns are common in childhood but disappear as people become more cautious about expressing themselves in public. For instance, when was the last time you skipped or galloped? You just do not see many people over 15 years of age skipping, sliding, and galloping. Because complex locomotor patterns are less functional ways of moving through space, people who skip, slide, and gallop through life are generally viewed as silly, or, at the very least, not functionally oriented. What do you think?

by folding the lower legs in the air. *Pas de boureé*, French for "step of fluff," may have gotten its name because the down-up-down of the three-step weight transfers caused a ballerina's tutu to fluff as she moved. You will find many of these names shared among dance styles. This can make your life easier as a student. As you begin to recognize familiar locomotor patterns, whether basic or complex, you will not have to worry so much about learning how the weight is being transferred and can quickly focus on more subtle shadings of movement, such as timing, focus, and direction.

## Moving in One Place

Remember your chair-to-door sequence? Repeat the sequence you just made with one addition: Instead of moving from one place to the next, find three places in your sequence where you will move, not *through* space, but *in one place*. Movements which occur on a fixed base are called *axial* movements. By developing your eye for basic locomotor patterns and combinations, you will find that it becomes easier to read movements that travel through space. Likewise, your understanding of some of the principles of axial movement will help you read and reproduce movements in which the body does not move through space but rather moves on or around a point in space that does not change.

## Basic Axial Movement

When we talk about axial movement we refer to movements which occur on or around an axis. You already know a few things about the concept of an axis. An axis has a fixed point, and, using the earth as an example, the fixed point is the center of the planet around which the earth rotates. To begin this chapter we looked at movements which occur through space, which, to continue the analogy, would be like the earth moving around the sun. Now we are going to look at movements that occur *in* space, which would be like the rotation of the earth on its axis.

Take a pencil and stand it on its point. What movements are possible without moving the point from its place? The pencil experiment can give you a good idea of the human body as an axis that can lean in 360° around the fixed point—the standing base. Because it is rigid, the pencil can only lean or rotate on its fixed base. Let us create an axis that is more flexible. Find three paper clips, and hook them together to make a chain. Hold the chain over the center of the grid below. The grid is labeled to make you consider the chain as a body that is standing on one spot.

Front

Left        Right

Back

Experiment with actions of the chain that can be accomplished without moving the axis off the center point. Be aware of how you have to support the parts of the chain in order to make the whole shape bend, twist, shrink, or stretch. What other movements are possible with this chain? What movement is possible if you pull the chain very tight and tall, and you do not allow the top to move (not even a millimeter)? What happens if you allow some flexibility among the clips but still maintain the vertical shape? Although the proportions are not quite exact, imagine that your body is like those paper clips; your legs are the lowest clip, your hips are the middle clip, and your waist, middle spine, and upper spine are the top clip. Play with the clips to create a series of four actions that go off and return to vertical. Get up and feel these axial movements in your own body. Find the fixed point in each one.

## Finding the Fixed Point

Fixed means set or stationary. When you were experimenting with the movement possibilities of the pencil, the fixed point was the end of the pencil touching the paper. Once you started working with the string of paper clips, you could decide if the fixed point was at the bottom, middle, or the top of the chain.

Finding the fixed point within an axial movement will allow you to be specific about how you are making or supporting a shape. As you probably discovered in this last experiment, some joints allow more options for movement than others. The joints of the spine allow you a great deal of axial movement options.

Take a few minutes and explore the options available in specific parts of your spine. Begin by establishing the point at the base of your neck as the fixed point. How can you twist, bend, and stretch your neck without moving from the shoulders down? Now move that fixed point lower, to just below your ribs. Giving yourself total freedom above this point, what movement is possible? What movement is possible if you keep this bottom point fixed and also fix the first base-of-neck point? This only allows you to move your ribs. Can you make this isolation interesting?

## Space Hold and Body Hold

These concepts, space (or place) hold and body hold, are useful to a beginning dancer because they can help the dancer to read and to reproduce movement patterns and shapes. During the pencil experiment the fixed point was the tip of the pencil. That was the part that was fixed in place, and the rest of the pencil moved around that place. If you were to fix one leg on a point on the floor and then fall in every possible direction without moving that foot, you would be moving with your leg fixed in space. This is fairly easy to feel when the fixed point is on the ground, but what about when it is fixed in the air?

Try these experiments to get a sense of space hold:

> Hold your arm in front of you, and, leaving your arm just where it is, see what kinds of movement are possible with the rest of your body.
>
> Now explore the movements that are possible if you only fix your hand in space.
>
> Now explore your range of movements if you put a space hold on a foot in the air.
>
> What kind of dance can you make by putting a space hold on your head and moving the rest of your body? Remember, space hold means fixed in space—no level or direction change for that fixed part.

If a space hold means that some part of your body is fixed in space and does not change, what do you think a body hold would be? A body hold is an act of maintaining the position of one body part relative to another body part while the rest of the body moves through space. It is better to learn this by doing rather than by sitting and reading. Try this experiment:

> Stand up and point your nose in the same direction as your toes. Now turn your head so that your nose is over your right shoulder. No matter what, do not change that relationship of your nose to your shoulder. Walk in a circle to the left. Lower to the floor then lie down on your back. Roll over to your stomach and come to your knees. Move your right shoulder to twist, to bend. As long as you keep that nose-to-shoulder relationship, you have a body hold.

Knowing what a body hold is can be very useful to recognize patterns and shapes in dance and to recreate these patterns and shapes yourself. For some people it is very easy to learn movement using guides outside the body. Others find it easier to use their own bodies as a reference. Do you know which comes more easily to you?

Whether you are moving in space using locomotor patterns or using all your joints to make interesting shapes on one spot, you are applying your natural, human abilities to combine what you know about gravity, tension, and relaxation to make a pattern of movement challenging to you or inspiring to others. Whether you are moving through space or in place, you are using the elements of dance that we talked about in the previous chapter. The pleasure or satisfaction that this activity brings you will have a lot to do with your appreciation of your physical capabilities. That pleasure or satisfaction will also depend on what you find challenging or inspiring in the movement of others.

Earlier in this chapter we likened the dance instrument, the body, to other instruments, and we stressed that the more familiar the musician is with the instrument, the more likely it will be that the sounds produced are pleasing. Your job is to become familiar with your capabilities as a moving body and as an interpreter of movement so that the dance that you bring to life is as pleasing as possible to you.

Understanding the difference between moving through space and moving in place is important for developing self-control and movement clarity. We have seen that there is an infinite variety of ways one can move through space and in place.

## Realizing the Potential of Your Instrument

It is important to understand both the potential and the limits of your instrument so that you can learn to challenge yourself appropriately and make the most of the instrument you are.

No matter how talented and dedicated a pianist might be, he will never get a piano to sound like a tuba. Likewise, not even the most talented tuba player will be able to make her tuba sound like a piano. How wonderful that both of these sounds exist in the world! How wonderful that each musician strives to bring out the unique character of the instrument.

### Anatomical Considerations

Different people are built in different ways. Bones have different lengths, ligaments that connect the bones have different lengths, and muscles that make movement have different lengths and varying strengths. Some people can easily hold a leg in front of their chest but have little side extension, can touch their toes with straight legs, can touch their chin to their chest, or can curl their tongues; others cannot perform these movements.

It is possible to make some changes in our physical capabilities through training. However, like trying to make a piano sound like a tuba, some differences between instruments need to be celebrated rather than fought.

### Functional Considerations

Bear in mind this question as you pursue your relationship to dance and movement training: What do I want from this? If you have hopes of becoming a professional ballet dancer, your training goals and regimen need to be very different than if your hopes were only as specific as the desire to become more coordinated. As with learning to play the piano, if you expect to be able to read music and play "Heart and Soul" from memory, your training will not need to include hours of scale practice and years of diligent repetition. However, if you hope to be able to interpret the masters, your training must approach not only the level but also the nature of their training. If it is your goal to play a piece by Liszt as well as Liszt himself played the piece over 100 years before, then, to prepare for such comparison, you must train in a comparable manner. If it is your goal to dance the role of the dying swan in "Swan Lake" as well as Margot Fonteyn did 40 years ago, then, to prepare for such comparison, you must train in a comparable manner.

Competition and comparison can be motivating factors in a person's training. As with sports, if you know what time you have to beat, you have some idea both if that time is within your reach and how you might wisely reach the goal. It is unfortunately frequent in dance education that competition and comparison become ruinous tendencies which keep students from realizing their unique potential. Dance training is not a race. As you pursue your movement training, continuously clarify how that training both suits you and serves you. Keep yourself open to new physical challenges and use the achievements of others as resources and inspiration. Learn to be a resource and an inspiration to others, not by mirroring or besting their efforts, but by identifying and developing your own potential. To that end, let us turn now to some basic anatomy that will help you.

## Basic Anatomy

You do not need to have a degree in anatomy in order to be able to apply some common sense to your movement training. The human body is an absolutely incredible entity worthy of a lifetime of study, but we are going to limit ourselves to basic talk about bones, muscles, and joints. We will look at 15 different muscles and muscle groups and talk about functional alignment and injury prevention.

As with learning to play the piano, it can be useful to know how the sound is produced so that you can maintain your piano properly and play it with sensitivity. If you want to do extraordinary movements like flips, splits, back bends, and high kicks, you need first to understand your human limits, so that you know how to train your instrument specifically and safely and you know what it is about those movements that is attractive or valuable to you to make that training both feasible and worthwhile. Bones, muscles, and joints support your body against the pull of gravity. In addition to providing structure, bones provide boxes which protect the vital organs of your body. Muscles and ligaments hold all the bones together; ligaments do the primary stabilizing, and muscles actually move the bones by contracting. All movement occurs at joints. Because of the different joint structures, different joints allow different lines of movement.

## Bones

The adult human skeleton has approximately 199 bones. The skeletal system is divisible into two parts. The axial skeleton consists of the bones which comprise the skull and face (22 bones), the trunk (26 bones), and the thorax or chest (25 bones). The axial skeleton is the axis of the body.

The appendicular skeleton is comprised of the bones of the upper and lower body which are attached either to the spine or to bones that are distal (as in farther away from the spine). These bones move our arms and legs (Figure 3.2).

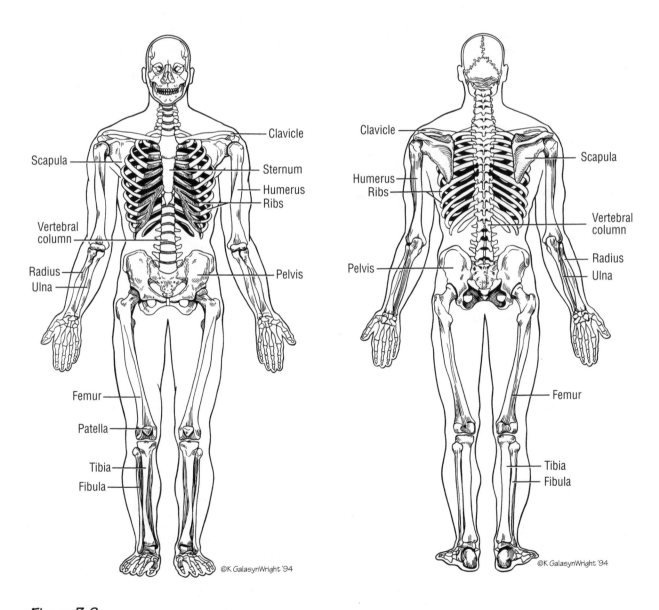

### Figure 3.2

Front and back view of an adult human skeleton.  © K. Galasyn-Wright, Champaign, IL, 1994.

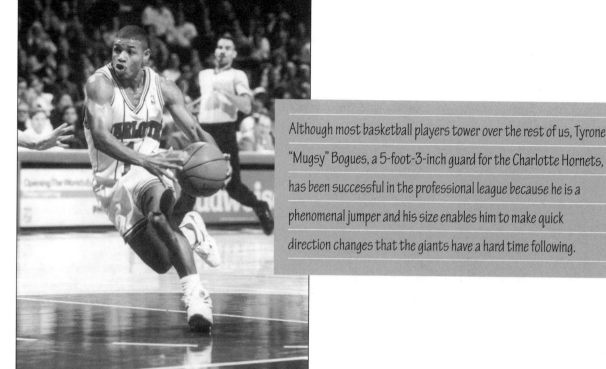

Although most basketball players tower over the rest of us, Tyrone "Mugsy" Bogues, a 5-foot-3-inch guard for the Charlotte Hornets, has been successful in the professional league because he is a phenomenal jumper and his size enables him to make quick direction changes that the giants have a hard time following.

The structure of each of these bones—their relative lengths and strengths—provides important variables when it comes to determining movement potential. For instance, a person with long toes (relative to the rest of the bones) is likely to be a good jumper. A person with a wide pelvis (relative to the rest of the bones) is likely to be good at quick direction changes.

## Muscles

All muscles, shown in Figure 3.3, move bones by producing three actions:

1. Extension
2. Flexion
3. Rotation

Assuming you are sitting down, we will use the hip joint as an example. Slump so that your pelvis tips back toward your spine. Now sit up straight. That act of sitting up straight, bringing the lower spine into line with the rest of your back, is called extension. If you were to continue taking your lower spine forward, out of line with your upper spine, you would be going into forward flexion. Slumping would return you to backward flexion. You could rotate this same part of your body by twisting your pelvis to the right or left.

Muscles contract and bones move to accomplish any of these three actions. Muscles are tissues composed of fibers grouped to attach one bone to another bone. The arrangement, size, and shape of these fibers varies considerably from one muscle to another based on the muscle's function. Muscle length and muscle strength vary greatly from person to person, so we are each endowed with special potentials for different tasks. Some people have relatively short hamstrings (technically, biceps femoris and semitendinosus) and, therefore, are not as adept at movements such as splits that require length in those muscles. Some people have very tight hip flexors, which means that it is harder for them to put their ribs on their thighs. People with long muscles, however, are often prone to joint injury because the muscles are less protective. You must remember that everyone's muscle structure allows both strength and weakness, and it is up to the individual to train in order to protect weaknesses and

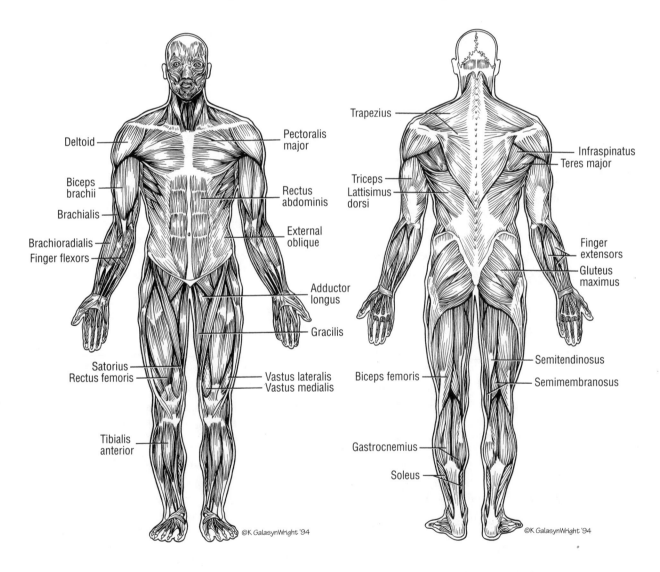

### Figure 3.3

Front and back view of adult human skeletal musculature. © K. Galasyn-Wright, Champaign, IL, 1994.

enhance strengths. Flexibility training will improve a muscle's ability to contract and stretch, but such training needs to be done carefully, sensibly, and consistently in order to be effective.

Both muscles and ligaments operate to connect bone to bone. Muscles, however, contract and stretch to produce motion, but ligaments neither contract nor stretch. Ligaments only stabilize.

## Joints

All human movement occurs in the joints. When you bring your hand from this book to your face, this movement occurs in the elbow joint. True, the arm moves through space, but the action is in the joint. Watch a mime perform the standard mechanical-person routine and, if the mime is good, you will clearly see this joint articulation.

Knowing where movement occurs can be very useful when training because it can help you to focus not on the outcome of a gesture, such as a leg lift, but on the source of that movement—the muscle action which produces movement in the hip joint. Once you start looking at movement from this perspective, you will be able to refine, simplify, and streamline your own movement.

## Accepting and Training Your Body

Your abilities to flex, extend, and rotate depend on the length of your bones, the structure of your joints, and the length and strength of your muscles and ligaments. You can train yourself to be stronger and more flexible, but you cannot train your bones to grow or shrink, nor can you train your ligaments to stretch or contract.

Accepting your body does not mean giving up trying because some physical task is difficult on the first attempt. Rather, you will want to apply all that you know to solving a difficult movement problem. You may want to specifically design a training program so that you will have a greater range of movement available. With work you can improve both your strength and your flexibility.

*Flexibility* is the range of motion in a joint or group of joints. What kind of flexibility do you have in the top joint of your little finger? That is, what range of motion is possible around that one joint? Now see what kind of flexibility you have at your wrist joint. What about at your shoulder? Go back through these three joints and determine what *limits* your flexibility in each of those joints. Flexibility can be limited by these things:

1. Length of a muscle

2. Length of a ligament

3. Contact with another bone or group of bones

Some of the limits that feel like muscular limits to movement might, in fact, be ligamentous limits. For instance, your femur is attached to your pelvis by (among other things) the Y ligament. This ligament will limit the distance you can move your femur

flexibility

straight back, behind your pelvis. If that ligament is long, you will have more movement than someone with a shorter ligament. This is a physical limit you must accept. A flexible back might be the product of long ligaments and muscles not only in the back but also in the front of the body.

Muscles stretch; ligaments rip. Through stretching and flexibility training you can increase your range of motion around your joints, but throughout such training you need to bear in mind that your unique physical structure may suit you better for some kinds of movements rather than others. If you have a short Y ligament, you cannot train or work out to add to its length. In order to imitate a position that has the leg straight behind the body, you need to find another way to achieve that height.

*Strength* is, technically, the power to exert or endure. Strength is measured by the amount of force you can produce with a single, maximal effort. Strength and flexibility are closely paired in dance work. Your ability to jump high depends not only on the strength in your legs and hips but also in your flexibility that will allow you to prepare for a jump by deeply bending your legs. Your ability to hold your leg close to your ear depends not only on the strength of your leg and abdominal muscles but also on the resistance or flexibility in your leg and hip joints.

Through repetition, gradual overloading, or pushing your previous limits, you can improve both your strength and flexibility and, thereby, increase your range of motion and physical capabilities.

Flexibility and strength are both inherited and developed. Through use and practice a body can gain flexibility and strength. You do not have to choose between being strong or flexible. In fact, you would be wise to develop in both aspects of fitness. A person who has inherited a very loose joint system will have more difficulty controlling their placement than someone with shorter muscles and ligaments. On the other hand, a person with loose joints will easily accomplish stretches and extensions while a person with shorter muscles will have to train to accomplish the same movement. Training is key.

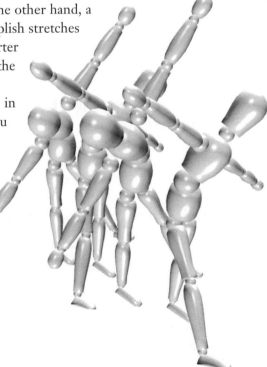

You have already taken the first step in developing your ideal, moving body: You have begun to explore how your joints, bones, muscles, and ligaments allow you to move. You will begin to identify your personal strengths as you continue this exploration (see page 44 for some questions to help you with this exploration). The moving body is an exciting instrument. *You* decide how to play it.

Before we consider the importance of the splits, flips, or back bends in your movement vocabulary, think back to the first section of this chapter and make a list of your personal strengths as a body simply moving through space.

Take a few minutes now to evaluate your basic strengths, flexibilities, and aspirations as a moving body.

The three most flexible parts of my body are

1.

2.

3.

The three most inflexible parts of my body are

1.

2.

3.

The three strongest areas of my body are

1.

2.

3.

The three weakest areas of my body are

1.

2.

3.

The three moves I would most like to be able to do are

1.

2.

3.

I am really impressed when I see someone who can

1.

2.

3.

Now think about the ways of moving you would like to improve. What kinds of challenges are you ready to set for yourself, and how willing are you to work, train, practice, or concentrate to meet those challenges?

1. Observe a person who is either injured or less able to move because of age or illness. How is that person's movement adapted because of a special, fixed point? Is that movement done to protect a body part or to compensate for a lack of movement in that joint? Explore to discover whether the person is using a body hold or a space hold in order to make coordination.

2. Create a short dance based on the concept of a body hold. Pick a body part, and explore the options you have if you maintain a particular relationship with another body part. Repeat your exploration using two other body parts. Repeat using a third relationship. Find a way to incorporate locomotor movements into your explorations, and develop your discoveries into a dance.

3. Create a short dance based on the concept of a space hold. Explore establishing the fixed point at different levels and different body parts (not just the hands and toes). Explore creating and dissolving these fixed points. Explore moving as a *result* of fixed points (like a marionette). Find a way to incorporate locomotor movements into your explorations, and develop your discoveries into a dance.

4. If you were to string 26 paper clips together, you would have an axis with many possibilities for movement! In fact, that is how many bones you have in your spine. The movements between each vertebra, each bone in your spine, is capable of the following axial movements: bending (flexing), twisting (rotating), and stretching (extending). Create a short dance based solely on the axial movements of your spine. Deliberately confine yourself to one spot, and explore as many movement options as you can.

5. Using what you know about different ways of moving through space, basic locomotor patterns, and complex patterns, create a series of four locomotor patterns that take you through space. Use two patterns that have even rhythms and two that are uneven. Each time you change to a new pattern, change your direction. For instance, you might take six walking steps in one direction, turn right and skip four times, combine a step and a jump five times in a row in a new direction, and end by going in a fourth direction by rolling three times. Remember, you have seven basic locomotor patterns to build with: roll, crawl, walk, run, leap, jump, and hop. The possibilities for combinations are infinite!

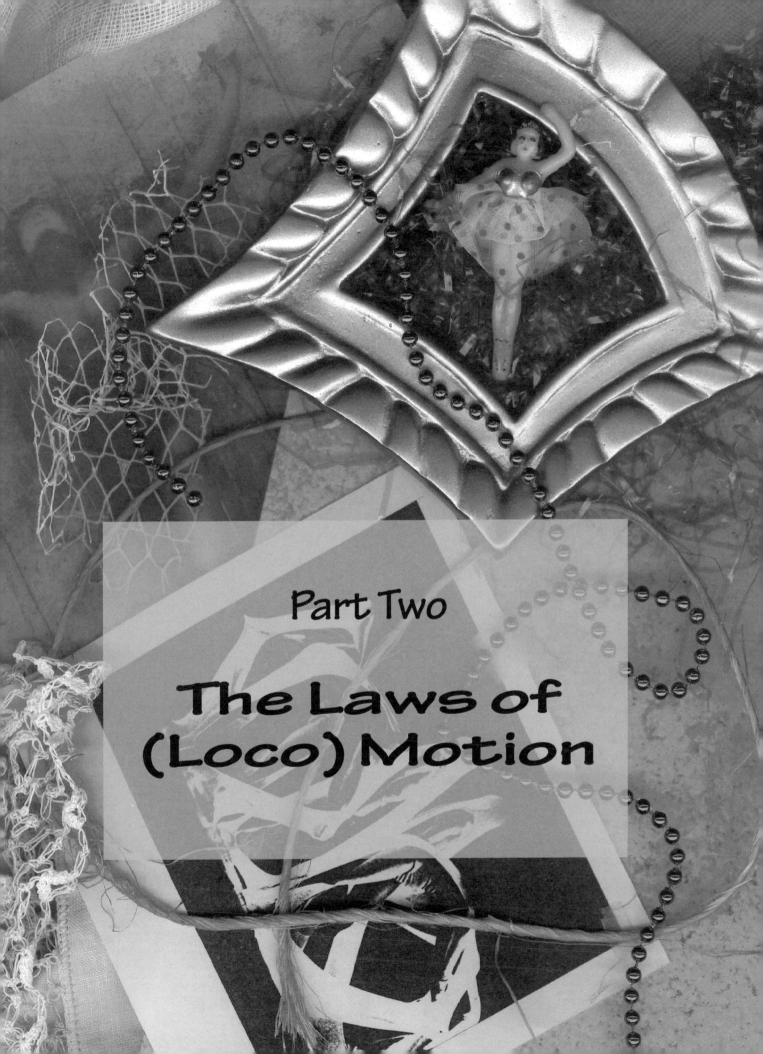

# Part Two

# The Laws of (Loco) Motion

chapter

# 4

# The Elements of Dance

As we mentioned in chapter 1, there are many similarities between dance and other physical activities. We differentiated dance from these by noting that dance alone is defined by four components: aesthetic function, intentional rhythm, culturally patterned sequences, and extraordinary nonverbal movement. In chapter 2 we looked at different ways a person might approach the study of dance; we noted that there are traditions as well as new options both for training and how to apply that training. We looked at the fundamental movement experiences that will be part of any dance experience. Finally, in chapter 3 we considered the mechanics of movement, basic movement patterns, and anatomy to help us understand and accept our physical capabilities and limitations. We now move on to consider the elements of dance, that is, the simplest principles of this field of study. Think of the elements of dance as analogous to the elements listed on the periodic table. Water is composed of hydrogen and oxygen. Without either, you do not have water.

Time, space, and effort are the elements of dance. The human body exists in time and space, and it exhibits some effort. At the very least, without the muscular effort of the heart and respiratory system, breathing—human life—would cease. A body has mass and occupies space. If you think about the fact that you are older now than when you began reading this chapter, you will recognize that time is also a fact of physical existence. As hydrogen and oxygen make up water, time, space, and effort constitute dance.

An understanding of these three elements, and the infinite variety of movement that can be created by varying each element, will help you not only in your dance-making but also in your dance training and appreciation. By looking at the ways you consciously and subconsciously manipulate these elements in your daily life, you can also begin to use your daily experiences as resources for your dance work.

## Dance Elements in Daily Life

You may not have thought about movement in this way before, but the elements of dance are facts of movement that you have worked with since you were born. Take a moment and consider the time, space, and effort of your movement—right now—as you read this book.

➡ Your chest expands, though only by a few centimeters, each time you breathe. The space you occupy, therefore, changes.

➡ Change your posture by sitting back, crossing your legs, or lowering this book. How much time passed during that shift? Could you perform the same shift more quickly or more slowly?

➡ Are you holding the book? Is the weight of the book partly resting on something? These are different kinds of effort. Are you using your neck muscles to hold up your head, or are you supporting your head with your hands, arms, and back muscles?

### Time, Space, and Effort

Think about your day in terms of the elements of dance. Do you spend a lot of time rushing around, or are you more likely to spend your days moving slowly or sitting still? What effect does the space you occupy have on you? Do you look forward to being outside? Do you balance the time you spend being observed by others by choosing to be where no one is watching your behavior? Do you rush to the door when class ends just for a change of scenery? How do you summon the effort necessary to stay alert in a meeting or a lecture that you find boring? In a circumstance in which you have a strong difference of opinion from those around you (or those who are in authority), what kind of effort is required to keep your opinion to yourself? These are all examples of how time, space, and effort are part of your daily life (Figure 4.1).

In chapter 1 we discussed the fact that movement is a response to needs, either physical,

**Figure 4.1**

Space and effort requirements vary depending on your daily activities.

mental, or spiritual. Walking into the kitchen to get a drink during a television commercial is one example of a movement in response to a physical need, as is stretching your legs under your desk or bolting from your chair for a quick breath of fresh air between classes. In your daily life, time is usually an issue. You are told how much time you will have for a test, lunch, a job, and so on. You are required to schedule your own time for homework, recreation, private time, and family duties.

Space is also an element of daily life. Can you think of an example of how your movements are affected by the space you occupy? How do the chairs that you sit in most of the day affect your movement? How about the designs of the rooms in which you spend your day? How might they affect your movement? How about the distance you live from school or work? Are you close enough to walk, or do you have to take a car or bus? Are you an indoor or outdoor person? How does the space you occupy affect how you feel?

## A Chart to Start

To get a sense of who you are as a mover—what your movement needs are and where these needs come from—let us look at how you use time and space in some of your daily activities. Begin by setting up a piece of paper with three columns, marked "Activity," "Place," and "Time" (see page 52 for an example). Under "Activity," list five activities which are part of your required daily routine. Be as specific as possible; instead of writing "Go to store," choose the verb that describes how you go to the store, such as "Walk to the store" or "Drive to the store." Under those five, list five more activities that are not required in your daily routine but are those that you choose to do. Now go back over the whole list, and next to each of the 10 activities that you just identified, start another list under "Place" that describes where your activities occur.

Look at your list again and notice what (if any) patterns exist in your day. Are your required activities mostly active or passive? When given a choice, do you engage in active or passive activities? Do you consider yourself an active or passive person? Do you consider yourself a small-space or large-space person? Do you prefer long-term or short-term activities?

The elements of dance are part of daily life because movement is part of daily life. When you think of time, space, and effort remember that these are not just dance elements; they are, in fact, elements we use to make our movements communicate the effect life has on us. What can you learn about yourself by considering the way that you deal with the elements of movement in daily life? You bring this awareness with you to your study of dance. Do you prefer slow, sustained movement? Do you always stand in the same place in class? Do you prefer to move by yourself or with another dancer? Do you prefer to move in straight lines or in curving pathways? Do you change levels easily (go down to the floor and up in the air), or are you most comfortable at one level? Do you move in spurts—moving very quickly and intensely, holding still, and moving very quickly and intensely again—or are you more comfortable with an even activity pace? Do you like to take risks when you move, or are you more comfortable moving with complete control at all times? Do you prefer to be watched, or do you prefer to dance just for yourself?

movement is part of life

List 10 activities that are part of your daily routine, five that are required and five that you choose to do. Then list where each activity occurs.

| Activity | Place |
|---|---|
| 1. Drive to store | In car |
| 2. Sit in class | At desk |
| 3. Change clothes | In locker room |
| 4. Wash dishes | In rear of restaurant |
| 5. Walk home | Outside |
| | |
| 1. Play soccer | Outside |
| 2. Practice piano | In living room |
| 3. Meet friends | In mall |
| 4. Watch TV | On sofa |
| 5. Eat snack | In car |

The next column we will label "Time." List how long you were in that space without a break.

| Activity | Place | Time |
|---|---|---|
| 1. Drive to store | In car | 10 minutes |
| 2. Sit in class | At desk | 55 minutes |
| 3. Change clothes | In locker room | 5 minutes |
| 4. Wash dishes | In rear of restaurant | 5 hours |
| 5. Walk home | Outside | 15 minutes |
| | | |
| 1. Play soccer | Outside | 1 hour |
| 2. Practice piano | In living room | 30 minutes |
| 3. Meet friends | In mall | 1 hour |
| 4. Watch TV | On sofa | 1 hour |
| 5. Eat snack | In car | 10 minutes |

Last of all, indicate whether your activity was physically active or passive using an "A" or a "P."

| | Activity | Place | Time |
|---|---|---|---|
| (P) | 1. Drive to store | In car | 10 minutes |
| (P) | 2. Sit in class | At desk | 55 minutes |
| (A) | 3. Change clothes | In locker room | 5 minutes |
| (A) | 4. Wash dishes | In rear of restaurant | 5 hours |
| (A) | 5. Walk home | Outside | 15 minutes |
| (A) | 1. Play soccer | Outside | 1 hour |
| (A) | 2. Practice piano | In living room | 30 minutes |
| (A) | 3. Meet friends | In mall | 1 hour |
| (P) | 4. Watch TV | On sofa | 1 hour |
| (P) | 5. Eat snack | In car | 10 minutes |

## Manipulating Time, Space, and Effort in Daily Affairs

We often manipulate the elements of movement without thinking about them, yet we do so to achieve a specific effect. Let us look at some examples of ways that you might direct your use of time to create a particular effect. You might humor a child by pretending to take a lot of time to think about the answer to a well-known joke. How about using the element of time to communicate frustration or drudgery by dragging out your performance of some assigned task beyond the time it should take? How about using time to express impatience by speaking in a clipped, shortened manner?

The sense of time varies with each person in every situation. Parents and children are known for having different senses of time when it comes to the telephone. Workers and their superiors often seem to have a different sense of how much time is required to do a job well.

We have touched on some examples of the effects of space on daily activities; now let us consider some of the ways you might deliberately manipulate the space available to you for a specific purpose. For instance, you might choose to invade someone's personal space as a subtle way of asserting yourself. In Western culture, polite social distance is about 4 to 6 feet, but if you stand closer than 4 feet from someone with whom you are not intimate, you offer a nonverbal challenge to that person's power. Have you ever had to sit next to someone, maybe on a bus or plane, who spilled over into your seat, hogged the arm rest, crossed his legs, and crowded you? Maybe you are the kind of person who shrinks and accommodates this sprawler, or maybe you are the kind of person who subtly expands to reclaim your rightful half of the available space (Figure 4.2).

### Figure 4.2
Have you ever used your size to intimidate a smaller person?

The beach can be a fun place to watch territorial claims. It is an unwritten code that each party should give other parties maximum privacy by setting up as far away as possible from each other. Perhaps you have had the experience of being one of the first to arrive on a giant expanse of sand. But as the day goes on, more and more people arrive, and the beach space changes from a broad, private expanse to a crowded scene. The space you had at 10 a.m. is entirely different from the space you are left with by 4 p.m. You can watch some people deal with this by moving their towels and chairs to expand their own turf, or maybe they turn up their stereos to aurally impinge on other people's space. Like one's sense of time, the sense of space, the need for a lot of space, or the need for a little space will vary for each person.

We can manipulate the elements of effort for a specific effect. Can you think of a time when you appeared to exert more effort than you actually were exerting? How about when the teacher is going to call on someone, and you deliberately display signs of deep concentration and effort even though you have no idea what is being discussed? Even if these examples do not describe your behavior, you may observe them in others. We intuitively use the three elements of dance in our daily lives.

## Applying Elements to Dance Training and Choreography

With what you already know about movement, you can use the elements of dance to describe familiar movement, analyze new movement, and create original choreography.

### Recognizing the Familiar

Reading dance is a skill that involves learning to recognize certain signs and symbols. Obviously, one difference between reading a dance and reading a book is that, if you are unfamiliar with a word in a book, at least the book stays in one place while you go look up the new word; if you encounter a new sign or symbol in dance, it is gone before you can do any research. Applying what you know about the elements of dance will help you read dance more effectively. Applying your intuition about the ways the dancer uses time, space, and effort will help you recognize what is familiar about the dance (Figure 4.3). Recognizing the familiar may mean that you notice a pattern of movement that is repeated; it may also mean that you notice that the dancers are continuously moving, that they appear to be drawn to one part of the stage, or that they rarely appear weak. Recognizing the familiar may mean that you see steps that you have encountered before, or that there is something predictable in the way that the dancers move. Recognizing the familiar may mean that the choreographer has chosen images from daily life—child's play, street people, bowling pins—and has put those images on the stage for you to ponder. The time, space, and effort contained in those images will trigger your memories.

Recognizing the familiar can also mean using the elements to assist your dance classwork. Whether you are using this text in conjunction with a class that emphasizes technique or creative movement, you will find yourself being called upon to read other people's movements. In a technique class you are guided through the repetition of

**Figure 4.3**

For hundreds of years, aspiring ballet dancers have repeated virtually identical exercises. We recognize these movement patterns and shapes as part of classical ballet.

certain movement patterns designed to improve your strength, flexibility, and sequence memory. In a creative movement class you may be asked to recall a movement pattern that you have created, or you might be asked to incorporate patterns created by other students. As you learn and repeat these patterns, try to identify what is already familiar about the movements and patterns being presented. You will find the learning process much less intimidating!

## Using the Elements to Analyze New Movement

Part of learning to recognize familiar movement is learning to recognize what is not familiar. I have seen this before; I have never seen that before. This I can predict, but how did they do that? If you spend too much effort trying to analyze a dance while you are watching it, you are liable to miss the whole effect of the dance. But afterward, as you recall the dance, it can be helpful to look at what you remember in terms of the elements of dance and to consider your intuition about how those elements were used.

Analysis is more necessary in situations where you are trying to master a pattern or sequence. You can use what you know about the elements of dance to help you read dance so that you can reproduce what has been demonstrated. In your learning process it may help to ask yourself some of these questions:

➡ How is the pattern structured in time? Is it all fast, all slow? Does it ever really stop? Is the rhythmic structure even or uneven? Does it ride or oppose the music?

➡ How is the pattern structured in space? What directions are used? Does it switch from side to side? Does it move from high to low? If it travels from one spot to another, is the path straight or curved?

➡ How is the pattern structured in effort? What kind of tension is being used? Does the movement seem to be bound or free? What seems to be important about the effort of the pattern? Are there accents? How is this pattern different from other patterns? How is it the same?

You can use the elements when reading movement and also when asking your teacher questions to help clarify what is intended.

## Using the Elements to Create Original Choreography

The cliché—there is nothing new under the sun—has been said so many times that nobody remembers who originally made the observation. When we try to create something new we have to acknowledge that we are simply reworking what we have been told and taught into the context of our experiences. The deeper you can investigate your experiences, the more you will have to offer as you create your own work. In terms of the elements of dance, the more you allow yourself to explore what you know about the time, space, and effort of your experience, the more you will have to offer as a choreographer. For instance, consider the experience of waiting in a waiting room. (What waiting room? You decide!) Think of this experience in time, space, and effort. Are you early or late, hopeful or dreadful, calm or nervous? Are others in the room calm or nervous? Are there enough chairs for everyone? Is there reason to focus on someone else in the room, and is this socially appropriate? Are you all gathered for the same reasons? Using your experience you can define the room and the nature of its occupants by focusing on the ways that time, space, and effort are evident. Never mind that there have already been dances created about waiting rooms; the circumstances that you create will be unique and valuable if you apply your experiences to your investigations of the situation's potential. When striving to create original work, do not worry about trying to be inventive. Focus on identifying what you intuitively know about the time, space, and effort of your subject matter, and share that with your audience.

When making a dance we use the elements to create a particular choreographic effect. Choreographers depend on an intuitive understanding of these elements when they create dances. Consider flamenco dancing. Whether or not you have ever studied this style of dance, you can appreciate that the dancer needs the skill to be able to create so many sounds, so quickly. If you were to study flamenco dancing, you would learn even more about the subtleties of the arm movements and the complicated rhythmic patterns, but even without such training you could intuitively sense that, while the dancer is swooping gracefully forward and back, there is a lightning-fast profusion of sound coming from the dancer's feet—a powerful force underlying the dancer's grace.

Similarly, a choreographer can expect some intuitive reaction to the choices made about the use of space. A Japanese company, Dai Rakuda Kan, opened their performance with a special ceremony performed outside the theater in which they would later appear. In this ceremony the six men in the company would cover their bodies with white powder, wrap themselves completely in rope, suspend themselves from the side of the building, and then slowly unravel the rope as they descended to the ground. The danger that these performers chose to assume was intuitively obvious to all those who gathered to watch the performance. The dance was slow, beautiful, and organic; it directly addressed the audience's intuitive sense of space. Or, for other examples, consider Trisha Brown's dance performed by dancers on several rooftops in Manhattan or a dance performed in a wheelchair. Would you feel that the time, space, and effort were different if the same dance were performed by an able-bodied person rather than by a person with a disability?

All movement occurs in time, through space, and with effort. We intuitively manipulate these elements in our daily lives to serve our physical, mental, and social needs. The dancer intentionally manipulates the elements of movement to create patterns of form or feeling. By consciously manipulating the three elements, it is possible to produce an infinite variety of movement. These movements may be familiar, purely sculptural, or dramatic. Others are consciously designed, spontaneous, or natural. Some can only be executed after years of training.

The elements of movement can be useful to anyone interested in recognizing, analyzing, or creating movement.

## Think About It

1. Try to design a movement sequence that moves through space, with effort, but uses no time. We have said this is impossible. Do you agree?

2. Using the elements of dance, make a snapshot description of each of the following: a stranger, a friend, a family member, and an animal. For instance, you might describe a woman walking a little dog as "moving straight ahead, stopping and starting frequently, with the dog providing slight resistance on her left side." The same woman walking a huge dog might be described as "moving in a zigzag pattern, lurching and resisting, always being pulled to one direction."

3. Choose one activity of your day, such as studying, driving, walking, or bathing, and find ways to investigate as many aspects of that activity as you can by exploring the time, space, and effort of that activity. As you work, allow yourself to leave the literal or real world behind, and discover other intriguing aspects to these heretofore mundane affairs. For instance, as you explore the activity of studying, you might get in touch with movements that pertain to feelings of anxiety and your inability to retain facts, or you might find yourself stuck to the chair or the books. When you consider driving, one look at the way that cars are designed will assure you that fantasy is a big part of some people's driving experience. How could you use time, space, and effort to bring such fantasies to performance?

# chapter

# 5

# Time

Human movement occurs in time, through space, and with some kind of force, effort, or energy. In the next three chapters we will look more closely at each of these elements, not by trying to break each away from the others to study it as an isolated occurrence, but rather by becoming more familiar with how each of these elements interact with the surrounding environment. These explorations will further demonstrate both the interdependence of these three elements and the limitless potential for inventive movement to be found by exploring each of these unique territories.

Each element has its own set of concepts. Studying each is a bit like changing from one pair of colored glasses to another. In the course of these explorations you may discover that you are naturally more interested in one element than the others. You may find that one element, one way of looking at dance, makes more sense to you. After gaining more familiarity with all three, you will find that dance and dance-making make more sense to you.

## The Basics of Time

All movement and stillness occur in time. It is remarkable how differently people sense time, either as a very precise monitor or a very loose construct. It should not come as a great surprise, therefore, to discover that in working with time as an element of dance, people have different preferences and strengths. Some are most comfortable working with music that has a very clear rhythm, and others prefer their movements to be

The Chinese believe that time is like a river—neither can be divided. This acknowledgment of the indivisible nature of time is built into the Mandarin language. When Mandarin speakers ask "What time is it?" they include a part of speech (le) that indicates that both the speaker and the listener know that the answer will be a rough estimate on a continuum, not an exact moment. How different this is from our Western obsession with digital seconds!

independent of a specific beat. Some are stimulated by music that drives them, others by music that allows them to float free of a beat. Dancers have been exploring the use of their own voices on stage in increasing numbers, using text, poetry, or sounds to accompany their movements. In such cases the structure of time is very different than it would be if they were moving to the sounds of popular music. Some dances are meant to be performed in silence; they leave the dancer free to speed up or slow down appropriately.

By now you may be wondering how, with all these possibilities, it is possible to talk about time as a dance element. These concepts will help us to discuss time: *tempo*, *beat*, and *rhythm*.

## Tempo

One consideration of movement in time is how fast or how slow the movement is. The speed of the movement is the tempo. When dancers ask for the tempo of the phrase, they are asking how fast the movement will need to be. Like many other words used to describe the element of time in dance, tempo comes from music vocabulary. There are words to describe very specific speeds in music. Adagio, for instance, describes a slow musical tempo. In dance, an *adagio* is a slow movement phrase which is often used to build or to display strength and control. Allegro describes a brisk, lively musical tempo; in dance, *grand allegro* describes a movement phrase with great leaps and lively movement.

## Beat

When asked to provide the tempo, the choreographer will respond by producing a beat—a steady, recurring pulse. These words, beat and pulse, are hardly new concepts. Your heart beats and creates a steady, recurring surge of blood through your veins—your pulse. What

Are 2-1/2 minutes a long or short time? It depends on what occurs during that period. In 1976, there was an earthquake in Guatemala that lasted that long and was responsible for the near-complete destruction of a city and the deaths of 23,000 people. In the dance work of Eiko and Koma, two artists whose work is characteristically slow, 2-1/2 minutes would not be enough time to turn the head from front to side.

We have the Italian language to thank for many of the musical terms we use in dance:

adagio—Slowly, softly

allegro—Cheerful, merry, gay

andante—Walking

tempo—Time

The French language contributed many of the terms we use to describe specific movements. These terms first applied to ballet but are standard vocabulary among other styles now:

battement [bàtman]—Beating, clapping (swift leg lift)

cambre [kanbré]—Bent, arched, bowed (back bend above the waist)

dégagé [dégàjé]—Release (In a dégagé, the foot of the gesture leg slides on the floor as the leg moves away from the supporting leg, and, at the last reach, the foot releases from the floor to point just off the floor.)

demi [demì]—Half (In a demi-plié, the heels stay on the ground, and the knees bend half of the full range.)

grand [gran]—Great, big, large, noble, majestic, wide. A grand battement goes above 90 degrees, and a battement is below that level. (In a grande plié, the legs bend fully.)

plié [plìyé]—Fold, bend (A plié is an even opening of the thighs accomplished by bending the knees.)

tendu [tandü]—Stretch (As the foot stretches to point along the floor, the gesture leg also stretches away from the supporting leg. The foot stretches fully but does not leave the floor.)

may be new to you is their application as dance terms. When we think of a beat, we think of something we can hear, for instance, a drum beat. When we hear several beats, we sense the amount of time between each of the beats, and we can then determine the tempo. Thereafter, we might or might not actually *hear* a beat to be able to keep in time. Often a dancer is required to *sense* the beat, which may or may not be audible. This distinction is important when learning about counting music. Try these experiments to be sure you understand the difference between a beat you can hear and a beat you can sense:

➡ Find your pulse by lightly pressing on the artery in your wrist or in your neck.

➡ Once you have found your pulse, tap that beat on your leg.

➡ Keep tapping the same beat, but tap audibly every *other* beat. You will have to sense the beat without making an actual sound.

➡ Keep tapping that same beat, but tap audibly on every third beat. You will have to sense two even beats between your taps.

If you now got up and did 10 jumping jacks, or some kind of exercise that increased your heart beat, you would find a different, faster pulse in your body. Imagine this faster tempo, and tap a faster beat on your leg, gradually working up to sensing this new beat in groups of four. (You will have to sense three beats between your taps, or TAP, beat, beat, beat, TAP, beat, beat, beat.) Was it easier for you to sense a slow or a fast beat?

## Rhythm

Were you aware of the pattern you made when tapping only one beat and sensing the others silently? This pattern of accented and unaccented beats is called a rhythm. You first accented every other beat and created a rhythm that recurred every two beats. Next, you established a 3-count rhythm. Finally, you established a 4-count rhythm, meaning on every fourth beat you created an accent. Look at this written out another way:

✔ Tap, clap, or walk in the room creating 12 even and equal accents. We will represent these 12 marks in time by making evenly-spaced marks on the page, indicating that the sounds occur at regular, equal intervals.

✔ Repeat your 12 beats *and* make one continuous sound for the duration of the 12 beats—sing a note, inhale, exhale, drone, or make whatever noise you want. Be sure that this sound can be sustained for the entire 12 counts. This addition we will note by drawing a long line through the 12 time marks, connecting all the lines together.

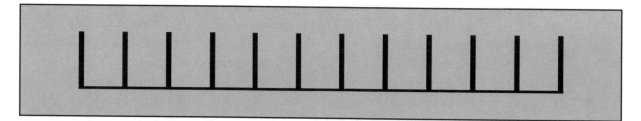

✔ Before you repeat your 12 regular beats by walking or clapping, look below, and you will see that an X has been drawn over 1 of the 12 marks. This indicates at what point and for how long you will make your vocal sound. The sound you add will only last as long as the time it takes for 1 beat to pass.

✔ Now it is your turn to decide when your sounds will occur during the 12 counts. Do this by making separate Xs over 3 of the 12 marks. Rather than making a long, continuous sound through all 12 beats, as you did above, make your accompanying sound when you get to those beats. Repeat your 12 regular beats by walking, clapping, or tapping, and add your sound during the beats that have Xs over them. If you had a long sound, you will have to make it shorter to fit in the time available.

Try these patterns:

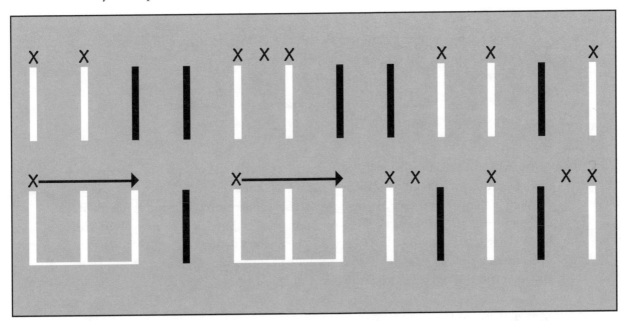

An interesting dance might be made by combining three or four sound-accent patterns and performing them simultaneously. What if one dancer made the "sound" of "Yes," another "No," and a third "Maybe . . . ." Can you imagine a dance with that music? What other interesting sound or word combinations can you think of?

In the exercise above, different sounds would be better suited to different tempi and different accent strengths. The "Yes-No-Maybe" dance might even change rhythm, that is, change the recurring pattern of accents, as emotions evolved. The appropriate rhythm for a dance does not necessarily come from music. Rhythm—a recurring pattern of accents—can arise from a number of sources, including nature, emotions, machines, and music. There are three kinds of rhythm: organic, metric, and mechanical.

## Organic Rhythm

Organic rhythm surrounds us—it is within us and is something we work with every day—but we seldom give it our attention. You may have noticed the way the wind starts to stir before a heavy rain. It picks up speed, the temperature drops, and the rain comes, first in big, scattered drops, then in a downpour. Soon it tapers off to a light rain or no rain at all. Only the leaves or other objects drip water. This build and decline is rhythm. It is an increasing and decreasing intensity that forms a pattern of accents over time.

Have you ever watched a trail of ants discover a piece of food? First one, then two, then hundreds of ants arrive and devour the food. Afterwards, the number of ants decreases, until no ants remain. This is another example of organic rhythm. Your heartbeat and pulse are also organic rhythms. Try this experiment:

> While sitting comfortably, become aware of your breath's rhythm—the rhythm of your relaxed inhalations and exhalations. At first, your breath may be affected by your attention. Sit quietly until you can merely observe and not interfere.
>
> When you feel you are ready, use the inhalation to expand your upper body, chest, and arms, and use the exhalation to relax your upper body and chest, and bring your arms back to your center.
>
> Experiment with increasing the range of your movement, but always keep your movement motivated by your breath.

You will probably find that as the work increases, the tempo of your breath's rhythm increases; this cycle builds on itself. Organic rhythms are rhythms which evolve through natural causes, such as effort or intensity. These rhythms almost have a life of their own. The rhythm of a lightening storm, the rhythm of a person involved with heavy labor, and the rhythm of a basketball player are organic. Organic rhythm is not measured in units of time that are consistent from beginning to end. Instead, the rhythm evolves or emerges from the effort required.

## Metric Rhythm

A parking meter measures how long your car has been in the space. A gas meter measures how much gas you have used since the last reading. A speedometer measures how fast your car is traveling. A meter measures how much and how fast.

The metric system is a musical system which measures time. Metric rhythm is not part of the metric system used for weights and distances in most of the world. In music, a meter indicates how the music is divided and how fast the notes must be played relative to each other. Go back to the tapping exercise to get a better sense of how this system works.

✔ Use both hands, one to accent the first beat and the other to keep the beat going through all 16 counts. Have both hands make the first beat, then continue to tap out the remaining 15 beats using only one hand. Play this pattern through twice. When the tapping hand finishes count 16, the accent hand comes in again, and both hands play to restart the pattern.

✔ Now divide the following 16 beats into 2 groups of 8. As before, use one hand to make the accents and one hand to keep a consistent beat.

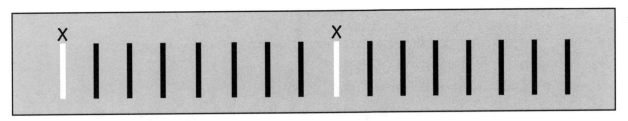

✔ Now divide the 16 beats once again, this time into 4 groups of 4 counts. Your accent hand will join your tapping hand four times.

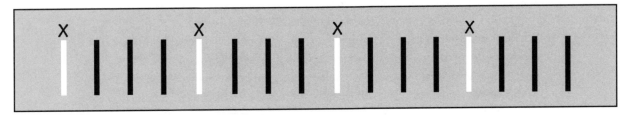

✔ Now divide the 16 beats into 8 groups of 2 counts. Your accent hand will join your tapping hand eight times (every other beat).

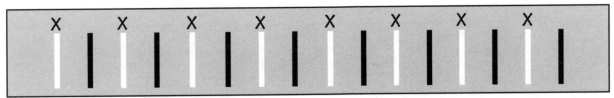

You have just played 4 meters of music! You have just divided time in four ways. Play each one through again, at least twice. Each time you come to an accent, *actually say* "One," and then sense or say the rest of the beats.

Meter in music is based on finding that "One." It is the place in time when you can hear or sense a return, a new beginning. Go back to the 4 meters you created above. Instead of letting your accent hand rest between accents, keep it moving like the hand of a clock, so that it hits the "One" accent at the right time and is immediately launched again into a new circle.

We have said that the meter tells you both how many beats and in how much time. Consider the second aspect of the definition (in how much time). In the first meter you had one accent, or one "One." In musical terms this would be called a *measure* of 16 beats. That is a long measure, and one not usually found in music. In the second meter, you still have 16 beats of time, but you have divided the time into 2 measures of 8 counts. In the third effort, you still have 16 beats of time, but you have divided the time into 4 measures of 4 counts. How much time? It depends on the meter.

Do all measures of 8 counts need eight sounds? Do all measures of 4 counts require four sounds? This is the tricky part of understanding metric rhythm. You do not have to actually hear the beat all the time in order to sense the beat. If a piece of music is divided into measures of 8, each measure will last for 8 equal counts of time, but there can be *any number of sounds* during that time. Consider an example. The following pattern is 4 measures long. Each measure has 6 beats.

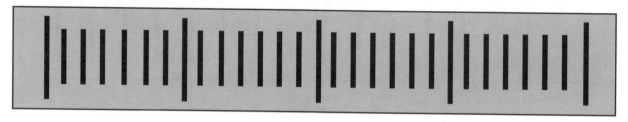

In each measure place a mark over any four of the beats. Make a different pattern of marks in each measure. When you have made your marks, play your pattern by tapping the marked beats and sensing the unmarked beats inside.

Add four more marks in each measure, placing some marks between the beats. You still have 4 measures of 6 beats, but you have a rhythm that has eight sounds to it. How are you going to squeeze all those sounds into the same amount of time? Play between the beats!

Metric rhythm is the description of how sounds are organized in regular, specified measures of time. If you study music theory, you will learn how to read music and how to interpret musical symbols that are used to indicate different meters. This introduction is not intended to make you a musician. This introduction is intended to help you understand how metric rhythm can be used in dance training and dance-making.

Dance is often accompanied by music, music that is organized into clear, metric patterns. By understanding how to count music—by developing a sense of the rhythmic structure—you will be in a good position to sense how your movements should or could relate to the metric rhythms in the music. You will also have the option, when creating your own dances, to design your movement to mimic or be independent of the metric rhythms of the music.

## Mechanical Rhythm

Mechanical rhythms are divisions of time that are created by machines and automatic devices. The ticking of a clock creates a mechanical rhythm. The clock never varies; it either ticks or is silent. The ringing pattern of a telephone creates a mechanical rhythm. When someone calls, the rings you hear are programmed to last for a certain time, and the intervals between rings are always the same. Mechanical rhythms are patterns which recur without any need for recuperation. Machinery in a factory produces an orchestra of different rhythms. It is the factory worker's job to keep up with the rhythm of the machine. The worker may get tired, but the machine keeps the same rhythm. Can you think of two other examples of mechanical rhythms?

It may help you to think of mechanical rhythms as rhythms devoid of breath, rest, or spirit. Humans can imitate mechanical action by eliminating breath, rest, or spirit from their execution of a task. For instance, if you were to mime reading this book in a mechanical way, you might move your head in a sharp, rhythmic way and turn pages in the same manner. This would be very different from your natural reading rhythm, a rhythm which would naturally allow you to linger or speed up, depending on what was on a given page. Perhaps you have heard someone play a musical instrument mechanically. They may have accurately played each of the notes, but somehow the whole rendering was less than moving. There was no spirit in the recital. Look for this subtlety in dance performances. Do you ever have the sense that you are watching trained robots or dancing machines? Look for this in your own dancing. Are there times when you are just going through the motions in a mechanical manner? Are there times when you might be trying so hard to do a movement pattern that you lose the connection to your own breath and spirit as you move?

## Using Time as a Choreographic Tool

Beat, tempo, and rhythm are all words useful for talking about the element of time in the context of dance. Variations in beat, tempo, and rhythm are all means of working with time as a choreographic tool. Going back to our definition of dance, recall that we identified four components that distinguish dance from other human activities. We noted that dance has function, intentional rhythm, is composed of one or more culturally patterned sequences, and displays extraordinary nonverbal movement. Two of these components are particularly pertinent to our discussion of the element of time as a choreographic tool.

We are exposed to mechanical rhythms every day, but we may not be aware of these sounds as rhythms both because we can identify the source of the sound and because the regularity of the rhythms makes them blend into a general background of sound. We may not notice the effect that these rhythms have on us. As a dance student and a choreographer, you should become aware of your responses to mechanical rhythms. Try this exercise to get a sense of the movement difference that results from working with the different kinds of rhythm we have discussed:

- Sit or stand where you have enough room to extend both of your arms in all directions. Allow your arms to rest by your sides as you focus on your breath.

- Gradually allow your arms to float up as you inhale and to return to your sides as you exhale. The longer you inhale, the higher up your arms will float, and the longer it will take to let them float back down.

- Repeat this movement phrase four or five times, getting a sense of how your movement is connected to your breath.

- Find a piece of music which is performed by human musicians rather than music performed by a drum machine or computer.

- Repeat the same movement phrase this time, working with this metric rhythm. You now have a sense of how music is counted. Try to find a meter that has a tempo similar to your breath rhythm.

- Finally, find a mechanical rhythm in your environment. Repeat your movement phrase by raising and lowering your arms only on the beats dictated by the sound. If you cannot find a sound that works for you, use a clock, and move in rhythm with the second hand.

Can you sense the difference in the movements based on these different kinds of rhythms? No one rhythm is better or worse than another. Each is useful for different purposes.

Choreographer Merce Cunningham and long-time collaborator and composer John Cage were adamant that the music and the dance be separate entities, that no relationship necessarily exists between the two. In fact, there were occasions when Cunningham's dancers would perform even though they had never heard the musical accompaniment. This innovation was a radical departure from centuries of dance history in which all concert dances were choreographed to music. Cunningham's contribution to the choreographic process changed the course of dance history and challenged choreographers to work with the element of time with a new kind of integrity.

## Intentional Rhythm

An alluring aspect of many popular ballets is how the dance fits the music so well. It can be very reassuring to an audience to be able to hear strong accents and see correspondingly strong movements or to hear a soft, lilting melody and see a correspondingly soft, pliant dancer move to the music. It was very common in the early days of ballet for the choreographer to attempt to make the music visual, that is, to make stage pictures that were analogous to the mood or story line of the music. The rhythmic structure that defined the movements came directly from the music.

Contemporary choreographers have been looking at their work in a new light and are not necessarily allowing the music to dictate the timing of the movements. Even in ballet (and even in classical ballet!) choreographers are now working with rhythms that have to do with breath, emotion, or effort rather than simply following the rhythms and accents of the music to which they are choreographing.

### Working With Music

Choreographing to music has its benefits. Music can be not only a source but also a direction for the statement you want to make with your dance. Consider the subject of love. There is no shortage of music inspired by this theme. Popular, classical, primitive, modern, literal and abstract love songs, symphonies, and other compositions exist to inspire the listener to feel the joy, pain, elation, sadness, and all other aspects of love. There is an infinite number of ways to dance about a subject like love, *add to the music*

and if you have found a piece of music that really speaks to you, that really touches you, moves you, or prompts memories of love for you, then you have a specific starting point in an otherwise vast sea of options. Once you have found your inspirational music, and you have begun to choreograph your dance, you need to keep a few questions in mind as you work.

How does the dance you are making *add* to the music? Unless you are using music with lyrics from another language, you can assume that the audience also understands the words; you will not add to the music by acting out the words. Does your movement go beyond the literal interpretation of the music?

What is the relationship between your dance and the music? You need to decide if your dance will follow the timing of the music, if it will complement the tone of the music, and if the music creates an atmosphere or a structure.

Also consider familiarity when choosing your music. You may have a favorite recording artist whose music you enjoy dancing to socially. This person's music would, at first, seem like a great choice for a dance composition. Think again. You and your peers have strong associations with that music—associations with movements that go with the music and emotional associations. How are you going to make a dance that adds to those associations and goes beyond them into new ideas? There is also a good chance that, when this popular piece of music is played, those who are familiar with it will be confused if you do not fulfill their expectations. These same considerations apply to the use of any popular music: classical, operatic, country and western, rap, or any other style. When working with familiar music, go back to these two questions: How does the dance add to the music, and what is the relationship of the dance to the music?

Working with music can define the framework for your dance—the speed of the movement, the build of the dance, the climax, the accents, and the tone of the piece. Is it dark and slow, or bright and slow? Gently sweeping or strongly aggressive? Music is also finite. Generally, when the music is over so is the dance. You can use the music to solve three choreographic challenges: when to begin, when to build, and when to stop.

The way that you work with the music will either be intentionally reassuring or intentionally disquieting. Suppose you were to work with a piece of music such as Pachelbel's "Canon." Not only is this is a sweet, harmonious, comforting piece of music, it is also a very well-known piece; you would probably be correct in assuming that at least a few people watching your dance would be familiar with the music and have their own associations with it. Consider the effect if you were to choreograph one of the following subjects using this music:

➡ A love duet

➡ A dance about the motion of a river

➡ A boxing match

➡ A stamping dance

The dances about love or the river would be harmonious with the mood and the timing of the music; they would be reassuring to watch. Dances about a boxing match or a stamping ceremony would be counter to the music and, therefore, would be confounding to watch. Done well, a boxing dance done to lyrical, classical music might invite the audience to see the grace in boxing or to be moved by the juxtaposition of harmony and brutality. Done well, a stamping dance might be used to highlight the eccentricities of a misfit or the frustration of an energetic person made to operate in a serene, civilized environment.

Working with music still allows you to explore your own interests in rhythmic structure, and it still allows you to make decisions about the duration of your movements. If the music is going "Ooomp paa paa, Ooomp paa paa," you can either "Ooomp" with it, or you can sustain your movement in a contrasting way. By making your movements either correspond to or contrast with the music's beat, tempo, and rhythm, your use of time will influence the audience's experience.

We have been focusing on music that is rooted in European standards of familiar harmony, melody, and rhythmic structure. There are, of course, myriad resources from other cultures that use time and tone differently. You would do well to investigate some of the rhythmically complex folk music of the world, some of the tonally diverse classical music of other cultures, and some of the sound fields being created by contemporary musicians. Work with music that is predictable to you. It can make life simple. But also leave yourself open to music that is new to you. As we will see in the next section, music from other cultures can be a good starting point for dances which either comment on your culture or help you to be creative when investigating established cultural patterns.

## Culturally Patterned Sequences

Folk dances use time in very specific and often very complex ways. Social dances typically use time in very simple ways. Whether or not you are a folk dancer or even a social dancer, you have still absorbed aspects of your culture's sense of time and might even be conscious of culturally patterned movement sequences that relate to time. For example, ever notice how people seem to have internal timers that go off while standing in a line? At first, there is respect for personal space, and those in line maintain a certain distance from one another. Then, regardless of whether the front person moves or not, the back part of the line moves forward, and the line starts to compress. This is that cultural sense of time in action. This behavior is not necessarily evident in other cultures.

As a choreographer you will be drawing from your personal cultural experiences, either replicating familiar and comfortable patterns or exploring and exposing new, challenging patterns. Your sense of tempo, beat, and rhythm is affected by the cultural patterns to which you have been exposed. For example, most of you have probably heard the loud, ultra-low bass notes of modern hip hop and rap music emanating from cars with high-powered stereo systems. While previously restricted to a few specific cultures, this rhythm is now pervasive and can be heard regularly throughout the United States. Note how often you hear this rhythm on the street during the next week.

Attending to the element of time in choreography involves developing an awareness of tempo and beat—speed and pulse. Attention also goes to the nature of the patterns that the beats make—organic, metric, and mechanical rhythms. Finally, culturally determined assumptions about duration, repetition, and balance need to be taken into account when assessing whether the use of time is appropriate for the function the dance is intended to serve.

## Think About It

1. Unless you are in a sensory-deprivation chamber, you are going to be surrounded by rhythms that have choreographic potential. Observe a tree in a light wind, and note the rhythms that are created by the leaves and the branches, maybe even the landing and departing birds and squirrels. Weave these into a repeating 4-count rhythmic pattern. Sit quietly in a room, and integrate all the mechanical rhythms you can hear in the building—clocks, heating systems, doors, and bells. Again, weave these into a 4-count rhythmic pattern. If you were to perform these as the basis of a dance set to one of Bach's Brandenburg concertos, would you be working with metric, organic, or mechanical rhythm?

2. Using five movement words, create four variations in time so that one is even, one is uneven, one goes with a selection of music, and one goes against the same music. Keep the sequence of the words the same; simply vary the timing. For instance, if your sequence was a step, hop, leap, bounce, and swing, you might first do two of each in an even rhythm, perform the uneven rhythm, start with a halting walk, hop and stop, do six quick leaps, a big heavy bounce, and a swing that gradually grew larger and larger until you lost control.

3. Take a popular song, one you and your friends like for dancing and listening. Experiment with making changes in the dance you usually do to this song by varying the timing of the movements. You are playing with some familiar movements, so, at first, this will seem awkward. Remember, it is just an experiment. Who knows? You might just invent a new dance!

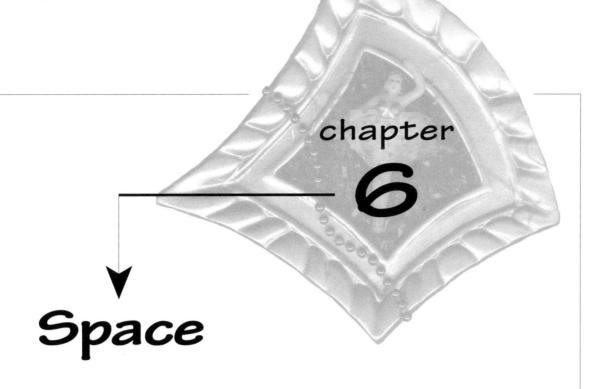

# chapter 6

# Space

**A**wareness of space—what you can do in it and with it—is critical to the study of dance. Dance is an art form that transforms space. A bare stage can become a beach, a ballroom, a busy street, a sculpture garden, or an infinite number of other spaces. In dance you can even create spaces that are fantastic, symbolic, or surreal.

Your use of space indicates what forces are acting on your body. Moving on one spot, moving as if being pushed or pulled through space, moving from low to high, and moving on a straight or curving path—all of these choices will indicate what forces you choose to show acting on your body. Where is your focus as you move? How does your size change or not change as you move? Is the space between you and the other dancers appropriate for the material?

In order to create the magical transformations of space that dance can achieve, it will help you to be aware of the components of spatial design. In addition, it will be useful to consider how you use space in your daily affairs—the different spaces you maintain between yourself and the rest of the world. This interpersonal spatial awareness will be applicable to your dance training, dance-making, and dance appreciation.

In this chapter we will consider six components of spatial design: level, shape, direction, dimension, perspective, and focus. We will also investigate the four interpersonal spaces with which we all structure our lives: intimate, personal, social, and distant. By understanding the principles that govern the use of space, you will be in a better position to deal most effectively with this element of dance.

## Level

If you were asked to make an opening shape for a dance (to arrange yourself in a still position that had some interest), what level would you be most likely to assume? Would you crouch low to the floor? Would you lie down on your back? Would you stand on your toes? All of these choices have to do with your level, which may be high, middle, or low.

Level indicates your position relative to the ground. Low is assumed to be below the level of the knee, middle level is from the knee to the top of the head, and high is above the head. These are not rules to be checked with a yardstick; they are general orientations for discussing level.

Some people are quite comfortable on the ground, some are happier crouching, and others prefer standing still or jumping. How low is low, and how high is high, will depend on your personal preferences and abilities. Obviously, if your work involves extreme level changes—going from very low to very high—you will be required to exert more effort than someone whose work stays at a low or middle level.

Movement at a low level often implies being rooted, grounded. A body lying on stage is a form that is submitted to the pull of gravity. You might see rest, death, sleep, or simply a horizontal shape. Rising up to a crouch, a crawl, or any version of low support still indicates an overall relationship to gravity where gravity is winning. The form is more down than up. There is still a strong sense of being rooted, of being able to use the body's center of gravity with great power. In the middle level the body has more options for movement, for quick direction changes, and for speed. The high level shows an escape from gravity; it defies gravity's pull by leaving the ground with leaps and jumps. In Western cultures this level is typically used to express joy and ethereal transformation (Figure 6.1).

*how high is high?*

*how low is low?*

### Figure 6.1

The high level shows a desire to escape the bonds of gravity. Natalaya Makarova makes flying look effortless.

In the past 100 years there have been a few instances of social dances that were done at the low level. One recent example was break dancing. In general, however, most social dances— most dances that you learn by the dive-right-in method—are done at the middle level. Why might that be?

## Shape

Shape refers to the form your body makes in space. Whether bent, stretched, curved, or twisted, the shape your body makes will indicate the nature of the forces acting on it.

A person stretched out on a couch makes a horizontal shape; a basketball player makes a vertical shape when jumping for the ball at the start of a game. Although each of those shapes indicates something about the person's relationship to gravity, neither one of those examples qualifies as dance. Recall that dance deliberately structures the display of the forces acting on a body. Those forces are made evident through your body's shape. Force will be perceived as perpendicular to the line of the torso. Consider examples from stage combat to understand why shape is so important. If you were to mime being punched in the stomach, the shape of your back would curve to show that force affecting you from the front. If you were to mime being hit in the side of the face, you would twist your spine and stagger backward. The shape of the body telegraphs the force to the audience. A skilled actor uses the torso to reinforce the drama. Likewise, in dance the shape of the torso directs the line of force which is reinforced by the shaping of the arms, legs, and head.

Shape is often a starting point for composition students. Working with contrasts, such as open and closed, wide and narrow, curved and straight, not only challenges creativity but also brings an awareness of shape as a rich, simple resource. Picture a dancer standing on two feet, holding her arms wide, and looking up. Slowly her arms bend, her head drops, and she becomes a closed shape as she sinks toward the floor. Just before she gets all the way low, she shoots one arm up and draws herself back up

Collect shapes from nature and analyze them for symmetry or asymmetry. Use the outline of an object (such as a leaf, rock, branch, or feather) to define a floor pattern.

**symmetrical asymmetrical**

and open to her original position. Just by using the contrast of open and closed, a dance is made. Just by focusing on shape, the dancer can make evident the forces acting on her body.

Let us use this same dance to look at the concept of symmetry. A shape that is balanced from side to side is said to be symmetrical. This concept of balance is important in dance because the shape of the body will inform the viewer of the forces acting on it. At the beginning of the imaginary dance described, the dancer was standing on two feet with arms raised high. This would be a symmetrical shape. If one side of the shape is a mirror image of the other side, you have a symmetrical shape. But suppose, as another dancer performs the same routine, one of his arms is bent, and he is slightly curved to one side? This would produce an asymmetrical shape; it is an unbalanced shape, and it implies that the dancer is struggling with the forces acting on his body.

Symmetry can be created with the shape of one body or several bodies. Two people leaning on each other, shoulder-to-shoulder, create a symmetrical ∧ shape. Such a shape connotes balance. How might you create an asymmetrical shape using two bodies? How does the apparent force change?

Shape, as a component of spatial design, is an important dance resource. Attending to shape requires that you are aware of the forces you wish to show acting on your body—the pull of gravity, the use of momentum and centrifugal force, the real or abstract picture you wish to make, and the effort or lack of effort you wish to show through your dance.

Imagine an empty stage. Imagine a dancer entering.

## Direction

So far we have addressed level, the position of the body relative to the floor, and shape, the contours that indicate what forces are acting on the body. Now it is time to look at moving the body forward, backward, sideways, and on a diagonal. These are the directions within which an infinite number of movement patterns are structured.

As a choreographer, the choices of direction you make in designing your floor pattern will enable you to reinforce the statement you wish to make. As a performer, your awareness of direction will allow you to execute the choreography clearly and completely. As a student, your attention to direction will help you to discover the patterns of movements required in a technique class.

Let us consider another sequence of movements in terms of direction:

> Imagine an empty stage. Imagine a dancer entering. The dancer takes four steps, then drops suddenly to the floor. He slowly stretches out on his stomach, looking past his hands. He pulls himself forward using only his hands, then slowly draws in his legs. Gradually he rises to a crouch then, folding his arms over his head, he runs in a zigzag pattern offstage.

Where did he start? Where did you imagine him to *go*? How big or how small did he become? Did he use a lot of space? Was he going to something or escaping from something? What kind of pattern did he make?

What space did that short description suggest to you? Could you imagine the dancer in a smoke-filled room or as a person on a battlefield?

Let us make a few changes here. Suppose another dancer staggers onto an empty stage. Right away, simply by changing the direction of her entrance from a straight path to a zigzag path, we have a completely different dance! Let us also say that she changes level during those four steps. By incorporating her level change with the stagger, we have also set the dance on a new course. Now let us say that she rolls over on her back, raises her face to the sky, and, as if drawn to the stars, stands and ambles off slowly looking up at the stars. Well, that is it for the battlefield setting, is it not? Likewise, this would not be a piece about someone in personal danger. We have entirely redefined that space because of these changes in direction.

## Floor Pattern

If you had ink on the bottoms of your feet, and you got up and moved through your dance space, your ink-stained feet would create a pattern on the floor. This is called a *floor pattern*. The space between your footprints might show that you went into the air, or that you took short, quick steps. A turn might show up as a smudge. A slide would make a long, straight line.

Your floor pattern is the design you make by moving through your performing space. The patterns you form will show the audience the statement you wish to make with your movement. In our example above, the dancer's path might be a straight one, indicating some kind of draw or urgency. Then again, the dancer could stagger indirectly, fall down, and grope around in a new direction; the dancer could also run off in yet another direction and indicate something very different.

A floor plan shows the journey the dancer will take. When you dance you outline a journey that has a beginning, a middle, and an end. There are three kinds of journeys:

1. Journeys that end where they began

2. Journeys that end somewhere new

3. Journeys that do not have an end, but by implication seem to continue (for example, dances with a fade-to-black ending)

Draw a square on a sheet of paper. In this square, draw one floor pattern that starts in one place and ends in the same place. On the same square, draw another pattern that starts in one place and ends somewhere else. Finally, draw a third pattern that does not have an end. Look at your patterns and decide what relationship (if any) these three figures might have to each other and what forces might be made evident by manipulating the timing of their patterns.

Your floor pattern will indicate which of these journeys is important to your dance and what happens along the way. Motion forward traditionally implies presentation, progress, and growth. Motion backward traditionally implies retreat, regress, weakening. Motion sideways traditionally indicates shifting, vacillating. Motion on a diagonal traditionally demonstrates gradual growth or retreat. The traditional aspect of each assumption is important to bear in mind because it is possible to work with these directions without hoping to conjure any of these dramatic overtones. However, as we will explore further when we discuss perspective, there are some physical facts about these directions that lend themselves to these implications.

## Direct Versus Indirect Patterns

When defining the space by choosing the direction of your movements, you are working with three options:

1. You can move in a straight line.

2. You can move in a curved line.

3. You can move on one spot.

Contained within those three options is an infinite number of possible variations. Where do you begin? On stage? Off stage? What is the first part of your journey? One long, straight line that goes from one side of the stage to another? A series of very short, straight lines that connect at right angles to each other (making an overall zigzag)? One line that only goes to the center, connected to another line that exits in another direction?

Spatial design has use in the classroom when you are trying to learn a movement pattern. Look to see what parts of the pattern involve direct or indirect movement. Spatial design is also useful for choreographing your own work. Direct motion connotes a different sense of control, purpose, and direction than indirect motion connotes. Indirect patterns could imply stealth, insecurity, indecision, even indifference. Direct patterns can imply that the forces acting on the body are stronger on the going-to side than on the going-from side, whatever those forces might be. Finally, direct versus indirect motion can be an interesting way to look at everyday motion—the floor patterns you make as you move through spaces, such as the grocery store, mall, library, even your own home.

Make yourself another imaginary stage space by drawing a large rectangle on a sheet of paper. Create a floor pattern that incorporates long, straight pathways with short, curving pathways. Indicate on this continuous path places where the dancer will move on one spot rather than through space. Turn the paper over and draw another floor pattern that incorporates long, curving pathways with short, straight pathways. Indicate on this continuous path places where the dancer will move on one spot rather than through space. Could the two patterns be performed as a duet?

## Dimension

No matter how big or how small, dimension is the relative size of the body, or the space the body occupies on stage. Dimension is one more clue about what kinds of forces are acting on the dancer. It is the difference between waving at someone by raising your hand to your chest and moving your fingers or throwing your arm up high and waving wildly.

You can look at the contrasts between big and small in terms of height, width, and depth. Just as your perception of level will be relative, so too your perception of dimension will be relative to other spatial clues. If there are five dancers moving in leaps and bounds all over the stage and a sixth dancer walks slowly, the contrast between the dimension used by the walking dancer and the leaping dancers creates interest. You could also create interesting contrasts of force by having five dancers walk slowly and making the sixth dancer leap and bound, moving through more stages of height, width, and depth.

You can explore the differences brought about by changing a movement's dimension using simple, everyday gestures. A wave, for instance, becomes something very different when the height of the gesture is changed or when the distance the arm travels forward and backward is changed. Choose another gesture and explore this aspect of dimension on your own.

Dimension requires variety to be effective. Without contrasts in these three aspects, one force prevails and can easily lose magical power. It is like listening to someone who speaks in a monotone; you can be loud and monotonous or soft and monotonous. Keep an eye out for ways that you can shade your definition of force by manipulating dimension. The magical use of dimension to shape space will help define the who, what, when, and where of your dancing.

## Perspective

A sculptor creates three-dimensional shapes with an interest in each possible view angle. Most likely, the sculptor is also aware of the difference that distance makes on the appreciation of the work and strives to find a setting for the final product that puts the work in its best advantage. The sculptor's challenge is similar to the challenge of the choreographer, with one notable difference—movement. When appreciating sculpture, the audience gets to move. When appreciating dance, the audience generally stays put, and the dancers do the moving. As soon as the dancers start moving, they create new stage pictures for the fixed audience to view. Bodies become larger or smaller depending on whether they move toward or away from the audience. The space looks balanced or unbalanced depending on how the dancers are arranged. Dancers appear intimate or remote depending on where they are placed. The sculptor works with level, shape, and dimension but rarely has to deal with the spatial component of direction. As soon as that aspect is introduced, you need to acknowledge that perspective is going to play an important role in the magical transformation of the performing space (Figure 6.2).

In *The Art of Making Dances*, modern dance pioneer Doris Humphrey discusses the magic of the stage space. She talks about areas of a performing space where, according to her, a dancer will be perceived as most or least powerful. She bases these opinions on the facts of perspective.

A person standing far away creates a smaller image that gets larger as that person approaches the viewer. Translated into dance presentation, the farther away you stand from the audience, the smaller you appear. The farther away you get, the harder it is for an audience to pick up details and small gestures. At a distance, the audience is more likely to identify you as a shape (open, closed, pointy, balanced, or rounded) than as a person.

You become larger as you move toward the audience. The audience has an easier time picking up the details of gestures, movements which occur close to the body, and facial clues. As a choreographer, you can choose to use simple facts of perspective to set up a mood or situation.

Look at the box on the next page and consider where you might place yourself on stage for the best effect in the circumstances suggested. Let us suppose you want to

## Figure 6.2

Concert dance in Western societies is performed with the audience on one side. In other cultures dance is often performed with the audience in the round.

appear afraid, and you have designed a rounded shape that is low to the ground. Would you place yourself in the center of the stage, downstage, near the audience, or upstage in a corner, near the back wall? (If you believe your answer depends on what the dance is about, you are beginning to understand the importance of spatial design!) Look at the stage from the perspective, or point of view, of the audience (Box A) and the perspective of the dancer (Box B).

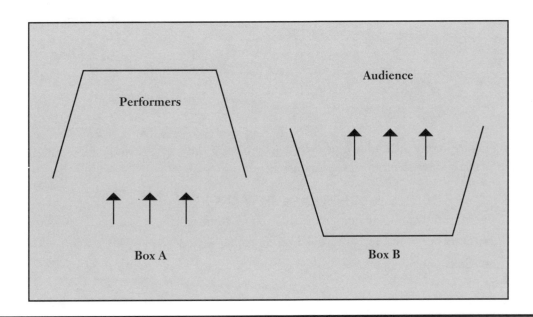

**place yourself on stage**

Where would you put yourself if

➡ you want to appear to be afraid,

➡ you want to appear as large as possible,

➡ you want to appear as small as possible,

➡ you want to appear powerful,

➡ you want to share something very personal, or

➡ you want to show something spiritual?

Did you find it was easier to place yourself on stage as a dancer looking out, or as an audience member looking in? Neither approach is correct or incorrect. It is helpful to be able to read a floor plan from both perspectives because not all choreographers will orient themselves the same way. However, when the terms stage left and stage right are used, they refer to the *performer's* left and right as the performer faces the audience (Box B). Given a preference, most dancers would start movement using the right side of the body, moving to the right.

Looking at the stage from the perspective that makes the most sense to you, draw your own stage space below.

Try to picture the floor pattern you would make or the path you would take to most effectively show the following circumstances:

➡ Start out weak and gradually become stronger.

➡ Start out confident and gradually become confused.

➡ Start out proud and gradually become embarrassed.

➡ Start out young and gradually become old.

Each of these progressions could probably be accomplished without moving through space at all but, instead, by using a combination of dancing and acting skills. Likewise, a floor pattern that takes the dancer diagonally from upstage to downstage does not necessarily mean anything. However, facts of perspective and the conventions of the theater can contribute to the meaning of movement if the movement is designed to utilize these two factors.

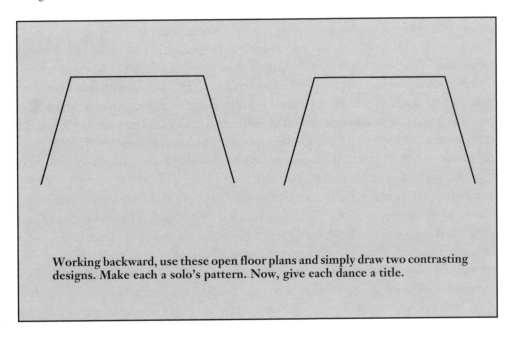

**Working backward, use these open floor plans and simply draw two contrasting designs. Make each a solo's pattern. Now, give each dance a title.**

## Focus

Although the face can be used without emotional reference, it is nevertheless one more clue to an audience about the nature of the forces to which you are reacting as you dance. Where you are looking, where your gaze falls, can be another important source of information to an audience trying to determine what forces you are presenting.

If you are looking in the same direction as you are traveling, you are indicating that you are responding to a different kind of force than if you are looking in a different direction than that of your travel. You can easily feel this difference by walking across a room and keeping your focus front, then returning across the room looking behind you.

Focus can be intimate, personal, social, or distant, depending on what you want to reveal in your movement. It is also possible to have a completely neutral face as you perform. It is up to you to decide what is most appropriate.

There is a special kind of focus that someone has when that person is in a private space. It is an inward focus—a look you have when you are deep in thought or when you do not feel the need to relate to other people. It is a look you have when you are deeply and personally troubled or touched. As a performer you can communicate this sense of space using your focus—the same focus that you use when you walk down the street deep in thought and the same focus that comes over you when some event has moved you and left you speechless.

There is a different kind of focus that a person has when relating to a close friend. You tend to stand nearer to each other than you would to a stranger, you might make softer and direct eye contact, and the muscles in your face tend to be more relaxed and responsive. As a performer you can communicate this sense of space using your focus—the same focus that you use with a friend near you.

Yet another kind of focus is used in social circumstances. You could call this your public face. This is the classroom look, the grocery-store look, the look you have when walking down a dark street at night. You make enough eye contact with those strangers around you to know where they are without engaging anyone in conversation or relationship. As we will discuss further in the next section, this focus is used with people three to six feet away from you. It involves both direct and peripheral vision. As a performer you can communicate this sense of space using your focus—the same focus that you use walking in a mall by yourself.

Finally, you have distant focus. This is the focus of celestial contemplation, also known as the spaced-out look. Your mind is elsewhere, not intimate or personal, and you are pondering universal thoughts. This focus comes over dancers for three reasons: They are afraid to look forward into the faces of the audience, they are truly overwhelmed by the force of the movement and its power and are having a spiritual experience, or the distant focus has been specifically requested by the choreographer. Any one of these is valid. The second option will probably read most genuinely, but the first has carried many a nervous dancer through performances.

## Developing Interpersonal Spatial Awareness

Let us look more closely at the ways you intuitively use spatial awareness in your own life. Edward Hall, in *The Hidden Dimension*, focuses on the animal basis of our human spatial awareness. It is a fascinating study that discusses how we are able to share the spaces we occupy in daily life, how we acknowledge each other's boundaries. These unwritten rules vary from person to person and culture to culture. The distance between bodies on stage may have very different significance to different people. For instance, some would find a dance using contact improvisation to be lewd and appalling because the dancers are in close, physical contact. Others find the dancers' remarkable abilities to share weight and to show an immediate response awe-inspiring.

This is a good example of how to understand the use of interpersonal spatial awareness when making choreographic choices. When learning to work skillfully with spatial design, you would be wise to consider some of the basic, human intuitions that apply to interpersonal spatial awareness.

Hall describes over ten distances that can be discriminated by humans in interaction. For our purposes we will generalize four separate distances and use the same terminology that we used when discussing the importance of focus: intimate, personal, social, and distant.

## Intimate

This is the distance from your skin to about 12 inches away from your body; it is the distance maintained when comforting and protecting. There is a high possibility of physical contact when two people are this close. It is impossible to see the whole body of the other person; therefore, each person relies less on vision than on smell and sense of body heat to judge position.

When we see two bodies in this kind of proximity we intuitively sense the possibilities inherent with this kind of distance. This is not to say that any particular relationship is implied, but it does make it hard for an audience member to believe that two dancers standing or moving in this spatial relationship are unaware of the intimate nature of their positions. As a choreographer you can choose to develop this tension by never allowing the dancers to look at each other or touch each other, or you can give in to the obvious and acknowledge the intuitively intimate nature of their spatial relationship.

## Personal

This is the distance from about 12 inches to 3 feet from your body, at about an arm's length. At this distance there is less likelihood of physical contact, but it is still possible. People in this spatial relationship can rely more on vision, but they still need to move their heads in order to see the whole body of the other person. Smell and heat are no longer good indicators of the other person's position.

Two or more bodies in this proximity can work from all three senses—kinesthetic, visual, and aural—to maintain ensemble (dance together). Their presentation implies accord on the simplest level.

## Social

This is the distance from 3 feet to about 10 feet from your body. No physical contact is expected at this distance. It is possible to look in another person's direction and view that person's whole body without having to move your eyes or head. One of the most interesting things that Hall points out is the "mandatory recognition distance" at eight feet, that is, at that distance you are socially obliged to acknowledge that another person is near (page 126). Dancers who maintain this distance on stage can be assumed to acknowledge this social convention; it goes against basic intuition to expect that two or more dancers moving eight feet or closer to each other are unaware of each other. What might be the effect achieved by requiring dancers moving in this proximity to avoid acknowledging each other?

## Distant

Hall refers to this as general space, but for the sake of continuity we will define 10 feet as distant space. At this distance the head appears small, the facial expressions are less likely to be effective, and posture becomes a more telling resource. Small gestures, such as wringing hands and shrugging shoulders, are less important. In terms of

*the importance of focus*

staging, the whole body has space around it, and, if the audience is about 15 or more feet away, it can see the whole stage space and perceive patterns and relationships of whole bodies. This is particularly important to beginning choreographers who may be showing their work in the context of a studio where it is not possible for the audience to be far enough away to see the entire stage. We would not intuitively assume that two people who are at least 10 feet apart have any knowledge of each other; it is possible to achieve a split focus at this distance and beyond.

## Applying Spatial Awareness to Dance

We have looked at six components of spatial design: level, shape, direction, dimension, perspective, and focus, and we have explored ways to use these components as a tool for learning movement and for creating effective choreography. We have discussed the application of spatial awareness in your daily living and have explored some of the conventions that address our need to share space with others in society. Intercultural study of spatial use reveals fascinating differences in the use of level, shape, direction, dimension, perspective, and focus. For instance, it is not uncommon in many religions for the leader (the priest, the minister, the shaman) to be in an elevated position, even if this means that everyone else has to be on their knees. The shape of the body is changed by the convention that stipulates that the head be bowed. The amount of space a Japanese subway rider is entitled to occupy is very little compared even to a rush-hour subway rider in New York City. In Tokyo there are mass transit officials who pack people on the trains. How we use space in daily life is certainly an interesting subject for thought. Let us take a final look at how you might apply your growing awareness of space to your dance study.

### As a Student

Now that you know about the six components of spatial design, think about how much space you need to move comfortably. In improvisational work, does it bug you to have someone right next to you? What level is most interesting or most comfortable for you to work in? Are you a low-level, floor person; a high-level, airy person; or a middle-level, move-ahead person? When it comes time to move through space, what kind of dimension are you likely to work with? Do you prefer to work close, within an arm's reach, or do you want greater use of your limbs? Are you a forward, side, back, or diagonal mover? Straight or curving pathways? And where is your focus apt to be as you dance?

When you are required to learn other people's movement, pay attention to the way you structure your use of space. Do you normally stand in the back of the class so you can disappear, or is this a good place for you to follow the maximum number of people rather than rely on your own sense of the demonstrated movement? Are you in the front of the class so you can see the demonstration most easily? Is this a good place for you to check out your own progress without having someone else's body obscuring your view of the mirror? Are you most comfortable in the front of the line so that you can control the space in front of you?

level

shape

direction dimension

perspective

focus

All of these questions encourage you to investigate the ways that you use space as you move in your classwork. Think too about your personal, spatial preferences and the effect that various spaces have on your daily habits. For instance, if your work space is very limited, the work itself might start to become drudgery simply because of the context. If you are a person who enjoys close interaction with other people but you work in a warehouse, you might sense that something is missing from your work.

## As a Choreographer

Now that you have an increased awareness of how you might design your use of space, choreography will be even more exciting. Experimenting with the visual effects of level variations, the sculpting of space by creating shapes, the calm of symmetry and the dynamism of asymmetry, the power of focus, and the potential of dimension and range will be aspects that you can use both as starting points for your work and as aspects that can hone your final product.

Think, too, about choreography going beyond the studio and stage walls and into your daily life. Your use of space in social settings may not be mapped-out by a floor plan, but, given a little attention, it might reveal some aspects of your nature that would not have occurred to you otherwise. Movements at a party, for instance, include some of our discussion about pathways and journeys. When you arrive, do you stay by the door? Do you proceed to the center of the action? Do you head straight for the food? Do you lurk about on the edges of the space or move in among people? Do you excuse yourself to go to the rest room just because you need your own space for a few minutes? If you are at a party where there is social dancing, where do you begin your dance? Do you create the space you need or respond to the space that is available? Your awareness of the aspects of spatial design has direct application to your studies of dance and to your creation of dances, but it also extends to a general awareness of your interaction with other people and places in your daily life.

**Think About It**

1. Think about the spaces that you occupy during the day. What range of movements do those spaces allow? This is a three-part exercise.

a. Go to a fast-food restaurant and observe the movements of the servers. Write down the sequences of as many of their movements as you can in five minutes of observation (turn, reach, grab, step, stuff, push, and so on). While you are there, write down your estimate of the dimensions of the space that the servers have to work in.

b. Go to a sporting event or practice and observe the movements of the athletes. Write down the sequences of as many of their movements as you can in five minutes of observation. While you are there, write down your estimate of the dimensions of the space they have to work in.

c. In your dance space, combine the two sequences. Perform the athlete's sequence in the imagined dimensions of the server and vice versa. Make a sequence of alternating ranges using one word from each list. Work with a partner to show a contrast in range. Make up your own dimension and range dance using the sequence material you collected. What would be the best accompaniment for your dance?

2. Some choreographers deliberately choose dancers whose physical dimensions are similar. Why would same-size dancers be desirable to a choreographer? Why would it be desirable to work with bodies of different heights, weights, and shapes?

3. How is perspective used in advertising? How are you, the consumer, meant to be manipulated by the way an image moves across your television screen? (Car commercials are particularly catchy this way.)

4. With another dancer explore the four interpersonal distances to develop a duet. One strategy would be to have a movement conversation—take turns moving and responding—at each of the four distances, and then choose the most interesting moments from each position. Another strategy to start from would be to devise a sequence of five or six movements and to explore the effects of the different distances on your sequence.

# Effort

**Y**our task as a dancer or choreographer is to find a way to demonstrate a wide range of physical effort. This effort is a combination of your physical, mental, and emotional powers, and the effort you display as you dance helps the audience understand the material you present. Are you trying to look like you are floating? If so, the effort you exert is different from the effort required to show that you are stuck or constrained.

When we use the word effort we usually mean some outward display of force or willpower. Think about what you would look like if you were pretending to lift a heavy suitcase. Think about how you would show the difficulty in resisting the temptation of a chocolate chip cookie. How would you show the difference between shoveling dry leaves and wet snow? You, as an actor or a dancer, could create these imaginary circumstances by showing different degrees of effort.

When a teacher criticizes you by saying that you just did not put enough effort into your work, that teacher means that some part of your *inner impulse* to do the work is missing. Maybe it is sloppy, maybe you did not put much thought into it, or maybe you had not found a reason to care about the project. Think of an assignment you have recently completed that you *did* put a lot of effort into and another assignment that you put very little effort into completing. What is the difference between the physical, mental, or emotional power you brought to each? When we talk about putting more effort into something, we are talking about approaching a task with more gusto, interest, or care. We are talking about applying physical, mental, or emotional power.

# Finding the Inner Impulse

In this chapter we will take an inside-out look at effort. Rather than viewing effort as a quality that is added to ordinary movement, we are going to see effort as action that comes from an inner impulse. We will look at effort as "the inner impulse from which movement originates." These are the words of Rudolf Laban (*The Mastery of Movement*, p. 19), a man who spent his life studying the relationship between the inner motivation and the outer display of movement. Effort is the combination of muscular, mental, and emotional power in action.

What inner impulse moves a lion when stalking its prey? What inner impulse moves a puppy to chase a ball? What inner impulse moves an ant to follow the other ants collecting food? Effort in dance concerns the skill of discovering and presenting the muscular, mental, and emotional state that shows the inner impulse or essence of the dancer's subject.

Some simple and recurring inner impulses are those that we spoke of in chapter 1 when we discussed the need to balance tensions in the body by shifting weight, changing posture, and changing breath patterns. The impulse to sigh, for example, causes a softening in the chest and a change in one's general, physical-tension patterns. The impulse to tense when someone stands too close for comfort is another example.

Suppose you are leaving a restaurant, and you suddenly realize that you have left your wallet on the table. The impulse to turn and rush back likely overtakes you. In this case, you will probably move through the restaurant with a different kind of effort than you did as you originally entered. Suppose it is a cold, wintry day and a patch of sun shines on your living-room floor. You might be moved to rest in that spot and to enjoy a few minutes of warm and calm. These are examples of action motivated by inner impulse. These are efforts.

In discussions about the elements of dance, you find that time and space are regularly named as two of the three elements of dance, but, when it comes to the name of the third element, you will find different names being used. You will likely encounter the word "energy." Perhaps "quality" or "force" will also be used. All of these words are right.

Use the word that makes the most sense to you. Use the word that allows you to think of the widest possible range of options. As a dancer or choreographer, your choices for controlling the flow of effort, force, or energy that you apply to movement are infinite. Your task is to explore that range according to your physical, social, and emotional needs and capabilities.

Sometimes audiences have a hard time understanding a dance that has no particular dramatic intention but is simply a series of movements designed to be visually appealing. The effort shown by dancers in such dances is, nevertheless, a combination of their muscular, mental, and emotional states. The inner impulses that drive the dancers can be disconcerting precisely because these impulses are not emotionally based.

Simone Forti (1935– ) spent time observing animal behavior and used her observations as a basis for several dances in which she applied the animals' uses of gravity, inertia, momentum, and impulse to her own movements. The following is an excerpt from her written observations, <u>Animal Stories</u> (found in <u>Terpsichore and Sneakers</u> by Sally Barnes):

Brown bear walk: Front limb steps and whole side contracts to pull back limb into place. Boom, boo-boom. Boom, boo-boom. Boom, boo-boom.

Giraffe walk: Back limb steps, crowds front limb which steps ahead. Boom-boom. Boom-boom.

## There Is Effort in Every Human Movement

There is some amount of effort in every human movement. The simple act of sitting upright in a chair requires some effort. Even while you sleep you exhibit muscular, mental, and emotional activity. The effort you use to block a net shot in a volleyball game will depend on the size of your opponent. The effort you use to get to a ringing telephone will depend on who you think might be calling.

Effort is the trigger that sparks human movement. We often think of effort as the how of movement, but now let us consider effort as the why of movement. If you needed to carry a child from a burning building, that effort would be very different than if you were to carry that same child to bed. Same weight, different reason. If you needed to leap across a stream in order to continue a hike, that effort would be different that if you were to leap the same distance on stage. Same weight, different reason. Even an action as simple as standing up when your name is called will be a different kind of effort in the classroom than it will be in the dentist's office. Same weight, different reason.

There is effort in every human movement, but only humans use effort deliberately. When you watch a dog digging a hole, it is clear that the dog is not trying to make it look as if the task were harder or easier than it really is. When you watch an ant dragging a bug twice its size, you do not get the sense that the ant is trying to make it appear that the bug is really very light. A leaf cannot change the way it falls so that it appears to be heavier than it is. Humans are different. We can use effort to create illusions. We can control and modify our natural human efforts (the inner impulse) to survive and to communicate. We use our muscular, mental, and emotional powers to dance.

## Forces That Affect Movement

The study of physics is all about forces. For our purposes, we will consider five of these forces which we work with most often and most deliberately in dance: gravity, momentum, resistance, inertia, and centrifugal forces. Dancers who understand and can skillfully manipulate these forces create the effort patterns that make their dances most effective.

### Gravity

You are an expert on gravity. You deal with gravity every moment of your life. Depending on your goal, the effect of gravity on your body can require much effort or no effort at all. A basketball player has to use much effort to be able to hang in the air to make a shot. A dancer will use a different kind of effort to balance on one leg. A person sleeping uses no conscious effort at all.

**In order to resist one force there must be force in the opposite direction.**

This truth is so obvious that we do not even think about it. But in our study of dance and the effort it takes to dance, this simple truth needs more consideration. Remember, we have said that effort is the combination of muscular, mental, and emotional powers. Read this law again, and think about effort in those three ways.

The secret! Those people who do amazing and enviable physical acts—like balancing on their toes, leaping to make net shots, and all sorts of other human tricks—have figured this out! In order to resist one force there must be force in the other direction.

Dancers live with gravity in a different way than most people do in their everyday lives. To know when to use that force to your advantage and, likewise, to learn to resist that force with different kinds of effort is the kind of knowledge that enables you to be as expressive and as exact as you need to be. For instance, if you wished to express a feeling of complete helplessness, gravity would be very useful. If you wished to express a feeling of power, gravity again would be very useful by enabling you to show strength through resistance. If you wished to express a feeling of weightlessness, you would have to work very hard to pretend that there was no gravity.

*Effort is the combination of muscular, mental, and emotional powers.*

## Momentum

Momentum is a property of a moving body that determines the length of time required to bring it to rest when that body is experiencing a constant force. The constant force is the power provided by the dancer—the power renewing a locomotor movement, the power sustaining any axial movement, and the power to start and to stop moving.

It is as simple as this: If you had a friend lift your completely relaxed arm then release your arm so that it would swing by your side from the front to the back, eventually it would stop swinging and come to rest perpendicular to the floor. If you wished to sustain this swinging motion you, the dancer, would have to provide force, in the form of muscular contractions, to keep your arm swinging. There is an infinite number of variations on how you might keep your arm swinging. You might recreate the illusion of the arm being lifted by unseen forces and suddenly released again. You might draw the arm along your side, reach to the front, and release into the swing. You might continuously provide just enough lift to keep the arm from coming to rest. These and other variations are examples of the inner impulse that indicates to an audience the nature of the forces being marshaled to overcome the ordinary physics that would lead to a predictable display of energy. Without a display of unusual, special, or concerted effort, the body in question would not do anything extraordinary.

## Resistance

Paired with the idea of momentum is the concept of resistance. Imagine a marble sitting at one end of a smooth-floored gymnasium. Imagine what happens when you give the marble a flick with your finger. It will roll in a straight line and gradually slow down. Eventually it will stop rolling. The same experiment would obviously have different results at the beach because the sand would make it harder for the marble to roll. In the gymnasium the marble encountered very little resistance, so it could roll easily. The sand provided the marble with a great deal of resistance, so it stopped rolling much sooner.

Weight equals resistance; the heavier the object, the greater its resistance to levity. For dancers, the more weight you use in your movement, the more resistance you will create, and the more you will be able to take advantage of gravity and of other forces related to your movement. To understand this physically, go through the following exercise twice, the first time imagining that your head is a heavy, sand-filled bag, the second time imagining that your head is a light, helium-filled balloon.

> Sit with your back long, so that your head is balanced over your shoulders. Imagine a slight impulse or a gentle nudge that causes your head to fall toward your chest. Feel the differences between the heavy and light versions? The sandbag image enables you to work with gravity, momentum, and resistance, whereas the helium-balloon image probably did not.

## Inertia

A body in front of the television remains in front of the television until disturbed by another force. Or, loosely translated into the law of inertia, a body at rest remains at

Momentum is a force that can be used to reduce the amount of effort a dancer puts into moving. You can experiment with a friend to discover some of the freedom that momentum provides. Stand easily, knees relaxed, ready to be propelled in any direction. Your friend will gently provide a push to some part of your body (as you did by flicking the marble). See what kinds of movement come from following that line of force to its conclusion. Have your friend experiment with different amounts of force. Try to discover what kinds of effort are required to follow each line of force. Change roles and observe the effect of the use of momentum by your partner.

rest until disturbed by an outside force. Our thoughts about inertia take us back to earlier thoughts concerning the inner impulse. Effort exists when the inner impulse brings us to action.

We must remember choice when thinking about inertia and human movement. A stone will rest on a path until it is moved by something or some force. The stone itself does not choose to move. Let us say that a strong rainstorm comes along and washes the stone to another resting place. The stone does not move as if washed by the rain; it *is* washed by the rain.

When we move—overcome inertia—in our daily lives, it is by choice or by reflex. The effort that we use to move shows what kind of force has disturbed our resting bodies. Our movement choices fall into two categories:

1. Moving because
2. Moving "as if"

Only humans move as if overcoming inertia due to some force other than a real force. Think about it. Can you imagine a turtle crawling along and suddenly choosing to crawl as if it were moving on ice? Can you imagine a cow deciding to walk as if it needed milking? We are talking about effort and what that effort communicates. Only humans choose to move, to overcome inertia, and to convey a particular effect.

Take a simple head gesture as an example. Start from a sitting position, back long, head balanced easily on top of the spine. Allow your head to follow as you twist your upper body to the right. If you twist as far as you possibly can, your head will move as well. Your head moves because of the movement in the back. Return to your resting position and experiment with the effects you can achieve by moving as if your head were not affected by the twist in the back.

Successional movement makes use of inertia and can, therefore, look very relaxed and organic. Successional movement is movement in which one part of the body initiates movement in the next joint. For instance, if you are standing tall with your weight evenly distributed on both feet, and you were to begin your descent to the floor by bending the top vertebra forward and allowing that motion to pull the next vertebra into the same curve, then the next and the next, you would eventually be standing while hanging forward at the waist. To return to vertical using successional movement, you would start from the base of your spine and uncurl vertebra-by-vertebra. With practice, successional spinal movements can appear to be the result of one impulse.

## Centrifugal Force

This is the force that propels a mass away from a rotating center. Perhaps you have had a chance to go on one of those spinning contraptions popular at amusement parks—the ride that spins around and picks up speed until the floor drops away and everyone is pinned to the wall by virtue of centrifugal force? Centrifugal force is of great use for dancers since it enables motion to occur in the limbs and periphery without using customary effort. For instance, turning quickly and continuously causes the arms to rise in proportion to the speed of the turn. The arms, if relaxed, will float up effortlessly to shoulder height. If you have got the balance to be able to hop and turn at the same time, you will find that your leg in the air will float up toward waist height, depending on the speed of your turn. You can use centrifugal force to escape the pull of gravity!

## Effort That Reflects These Forces

Part of dance's magic is the opportunity to create an illusion of force, effort, or energy. A ballet dancer balancing on pointe creates the illusion that gravity has no effect on the body. A dancer can sail through the air without apparent effort, or a dancer can show great effort to jump a few inches. The choice of what kind of force to show and how to make that force evident is in the power of the dancer and choreographer. We mortals cannot escape the laws of physics, but we can work skillfully and magically to manipulate an audience's perception of these laws.

There are four efforts that you can manipulate to create the illusion of force or a lack of force:

**time     space     weight     flow**

Look at a leap and consider the possibilities each of these aspects provides for manipulating the illusion of force in this simple action.

A long time in the air creates the illusion of a gravity-free creature. A short time in the air suggests more resistance, possibly more weight, less momentum, more inertia, and less assistance of centrifugal force. A leap which involves great elevation suggests that the dancer is more free from the pull of gravity than one whose elevation is slight; however, long, low leaps indicate a lack of resistance in a different plane—the horizontal versus the vertical. Long, low leaps indicate that the dancer has the assistance of momentum and is able to apply weight to propel forward. When we consider the flow of a movement, we are considering the overall integration of all of the forces that act upon a body—gravity, resistance, momentum, inertia, and centrifugal force. A dancer who comes to a grinding halt between leaps breaks the flow of movement. To break this flow the dancer might appear to give in to gravity, be overcome by resistance, or completely lose momentum. The combination of these four efforts provides the dancer with the means to make evident an infinite variety of forces acting on the body.

Time, as discussed in chapter 5, can be measured and described in different ways. Movements could be discussed as fast, slow, or something between those two speeds.

*create an illusion*

But as we look at some of the other adjectives that relate to time, we see that effort plays a role in determining how time is constructed or used. Consider several time-related words and the effort implied by each one.

**Arrange the words quick, gradual, sluggish, leisurely, sudden, and brisk on the scale below according to their being relatively fast or slow:**

Slow_____Fast

**Where would you place the word "endless"?**

Time is relative to effort. In order to say one thing is quick you need to have something less or more quick for a comparison.

Space is also relative to effort. The direction that a movement takes in space will inform us about the kind of effort being used. As we discussed in chapter 6, a dancer who enters the stage moving in a direct line shows a different kind of effort than a dancer who enters the stage staggering forward. In *The Mastery of Movement*, Laban discussed direction and use of space in terms of direct and pliant (or flexible) movement. Words such as poke, jab, punch, thrust, and pat describe direct actions. Words such as float, wring, glide, and flick describe what Laban would label flexible movements—movements which occur in a curved, rather than straight, line. What would you say is the difference between a poke and a punch? Both are direct movements; both are toward the fast end of the time line. How are these actions different?

The difference between a poke and a punch is weight—the amount of force involved with each one. Weight equals resistance. So, if weight equals resistance, then force, or, the amount of power used to overcome resistance, is going to be a factor when displaying effort. Strong force will result in a punch; light force will yield a poke. Use strong and light as the two ends of a line for force and weight. As we did with time, consider where several words which describe movement would fit relative to each other.

**Arrange the words slash, dab, glide, wring, float, and thrust on the scale below:**

Light_____Strong

The amount of weight or force used in each of these actions will both require and display a particular effort—a physical, mental, and emotional display.

The last aspect of effort that Laban discussed—flow—is the degree to which the action is either bound or free. Look again at the six words above. Which would you say describes energy which is bound? What about energy which is free? Movements which are bound are tightly controlled. The lines and shapes made by the body are sharp and defined. The lines and shapes made by a body which is moving with loose control are fluid and constantly changing—no sudden stops and starts.

Looking at the graph below, consider where you would place yourself in terms of a preference for moving with either a bound or a free style.

Free_____Bound

Toward which end would you rate your preference for movement styles you enjoy watching others perform?

## Integrating Inner and Outer Forces

Remember that there is effort in every human movement and that the display of effort makes evident the inner impulse in response to outer forces. Mastery of effort comes with being sensitive to that spark of inner impulse and being clever at manipulating the presentation of that spark in relation to the forces of gravity. The more we understand the interplay of these forces, the more we can use them to shape movement. To pull all of this together, consider a simple experiment involving only two actions: walking and standing still.

This experiment is an exploration of your options to deal with all the forces we have just considered: gravity, momentum, resistance, inertia, and centrifugal forces. When you walk, you may walk anywhere for as long as you wish. You determine the speed and direction of your walking. You determine when you stop. When you have stopped, stand still until you wish to walk again. Work with these two activities for at least 3 minutes.

This experiment has to do with feeling the pull of gravity on your vertical frame, feeling the inner impulse to overcome inertia, feeling the momentum of your falling body as you begin to move, feeling the resistance of each step and the necessity to continue to supply force in order to continue moving, feeling the lightness encountered in a swift turn, and feeling the inner impulse to come to rest again. Physically there is work to be done in terms of muscles firing, coordinating, balancing, and timing your locomotion and stillness. Mentally you are present making decisions about moving, directional changes, and speed changes. Emotionally you become invested in any number of ways. Perhaps you feel silly doing this exercise, and you are a little tense. Perhaps you are bored doing this exercise, and you are a little lax, not really being still, not really varying your speed or direction with ingenuity. Perhaps you are curious about your potential, and you are using this exercise to experiment with a variety of different movements, weights, and risks. Regardless of your approach, you will have some emotional response to moving with this focus. On completion, you will have a sense of the physical, mental, and emotional powers involved with the combination of these two simple tasks. Your own execution will have been a study of effort.

Now let us set up some physical, emotional, and mental challenges to discover effort. Use the following options—being still, turning, and the sequence of step-step-leap—to explore these three purely *physical* challenges:

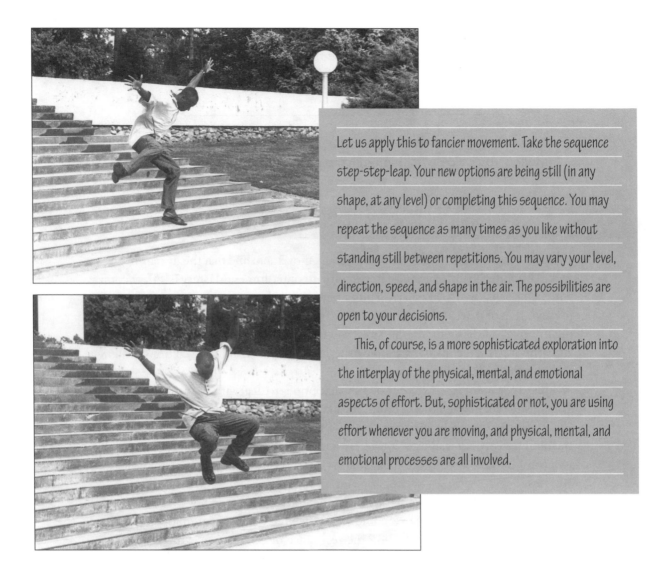

Let us apply this to fancier movement. Take the sequence step-step-leap. Your new options are being still (in any shape, at any level) or completing this sequence. You may repeat the sequence as many times as you like without standing still between repetitions. You may vary your level, direction, speed, and shape in the air. The possibilities are open to your decisions.

This, of course, is a more sophisticated exploration into the interplay of the physical, mental, and emotional aspects of effort. But, sophisticated or not, you are using effort whenever you are moving, and physical, mental, and emotional processes are all involved.

1. Moving as fast as possible
2. Moving in curved lines
3. Moving as lightly as possible

Now work with three purely *emotional* challenges:

1. Motivated by fear
2. Motivated by confusion
3. Motivated by joy

Finally, work with three purely *mental* challenges:

1. Complete the sequence four times within 15 seconds.
2. Complete the sequence forming the letters "O" and "U."
3. Imagine that you are a mosquito.

Can you feel that effort coming from within? Can you feel the forces of gravity—weight, inertia, momentum, resistance, and centrifugal force—as you work?

## Your Best Effort

We have been using the physical fact of life on earth—the forces of gravity—as a starting point for our discussion of effort. We have repeatedly stated that the display of effort includes not only muscular power but also mental and emotional power. As intelligent beings, we have the capacity to think, feel, and remember. We have the capacity to create from our experiences. We have the capacity to share our thoughts, feelings, and memories, and we have the capacity to hide them. We are capable of feeling one emotion and showing another. Dance is most successful when the dancer is totally present in body, mind, and spirit. When the effort shown is consistent with the physical, mental, and emotional intention, the dance makes sense. Consider a few ways that mental and emotional powers can affect the way we dance.

### Mental Effort

Mental power is an important aspect of effort which must be balanced by the other powers. Think of the contrast between a person digging a ditch and a person digging on an archaeological expedition. Each of these people will attend to a similar physical task in very different ways. Think of the contrast between the way a runner moves when training and the way the runner moves in the actual race. Applying this to dance, have you ever watched a performer who moved beautifully but who seemed to be not quite involved with the dance? It is possible to think so much about the sequence or the steps that your mental power robs your muscular and emotional powers.

Overusing your mental powers affects your effort in other ways. For instance, your breathing will probably be restricted, and your coordination may be off. A dancer's performance will be affected if the dancer's mental powers are out of balance with the muscular and emotional powers.

Try this movement sequence to see how over-intellectualizing can get in the way of a desired effort:

There is a total of seven steps. The first three steps travel forward, the next three turn in a circle, and the last step brings your feet together. The whole pattern moves in a straight line. Get up and try it.

Now repeat the pattern as you say the first seven letters of the alphabet, one letter per step.

Now repeat the pattern as you say the last seven letters of the alphabet, as Z, Y, X, and so on.

How did your concentration on tangential tasks affect your performance?

## Emotional Effort

Like mental power, emotional power can affect the effort a dancer both feels and displays. Nervousness, self-confidence, fear, and joy certainly affect effort. We have the ability to use our imagination to create mental and emotional states that suit our needs.

Children are very good at creating imaginary circumstances. That same skill is important in any creative activity, and it is particularly valuable to dancers. We can use that mental and emotional power to create the transformations we call dance.

Sit comfortably, and allow your head to tilt and hang toward one shoulder. Now imagine that there is a string pulling the top of your head in a high, diagonal line. Feel that pull, and imagine that the string is suddenly cut. Return to your position with your head balanced on your spine. This time imagine that you are straining to overhear a conversation that is just out of earshot. Suddenly the speaker enters the room, and you want to look as if you are dozing. Finally, repeat this movement sequence without adding any imaginative circumstances. Can you feel a difference in the inner impulse of the three sequences? Can you sense a difference in the outward display of the three sequences?

## Effort Is Compelling

Of all the things that make dancing so exciting to watch, the way the dancer uses effort is ultimately the most compelling. Control or lack of control, giving in to gravity or transcending gravity, and falling and recovering are all metaphors for the human condition played out through the dancer's manipulation of effort.

None of the three elements—time, space, or effort—can exist without the other two, but effort—the apparent investment of the dancer in the moment—gives the viewer the most direct information about the function of the dance.

### Think About It

1. Pick a nonhuman model to observe—an animal, fish, bird, or insect— or something from the natural world that is capable of movement, such as a cloud. Make a list of at least three adjectives that describe the model. Make a list of at least three adverbs that describe how that model moves. If the model were a cat, this might be a list of adjectives: fat, sneaky, quiet, delicate, and indifferent. Some appropriate adverbs may include: slowly, proudly, lightly, playfully, easily, or gracefully.

2. Next make word pairs by taking one from each list, and see what kind of movement is created. For instance, how would you move in a quiet and graceful way? What movements do you get from combining sneaky and graceful? Do these effort patterns remind you of any human efforts or situations? How do these patterns change if you change your mental or emotional approach to the movement?

# Part Three

# The Sense of Movement

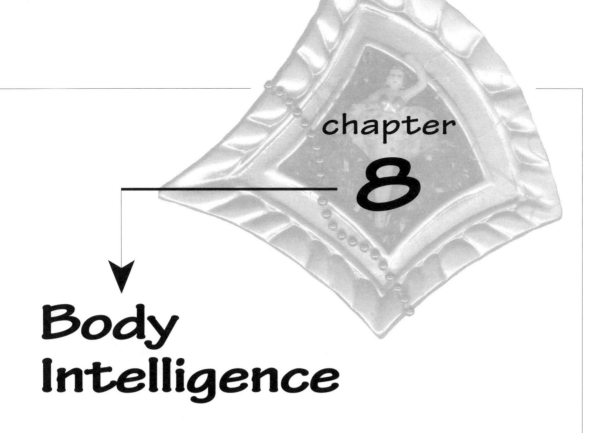

# Body Intelligence

**S**tudents are drawn to dance for a variety of reasons. Some want to get in shape, learn exciting movements, or become more coordinated. Some are drawn to dance because they like moving—they like being physical—and they think that dance might also be satisfying. Others come because they are dissatisfied with the way they look or move, and they hope that dance classes will improve their control over their bodies. The process of dance training can be a tricky balancing act between trying to change the way you are and trying to enjoy the way you are.

As you struggle to duplicate new patterns in technique class or rack your brain for a unique, inventive composition idea, you may curse both your inability to imitate and your inability to create. Placing your mind against your body ("Why can't I remember those steps?" or "I wish I could think up moves of my own!") is not the answer. A more productive approach involves discovering how your body works with your brain as a thinking partner. This understanding will give you insight into your strengths as a dancer and your preferences as a choreographer; it may stimulate a more balanced mind-body relationship.

The physical reactions, reflexes, and habits that are stored in your muscles as well as your mind make up your body intelligence. This chapter is devoted to a clearer understanding of the role body intelligence plays in dance and in daily life.

103

# Examining Intelligence

What makes someone intelligent? What names come to mind when asked, "Who have been the most intelligent people in all history?" Names such as Albert Einstein, Socrates, Leonardo da Vinci, Madame Curie, Isaac Newton, and Michelangelo might occur to you. How about Yogi Berra? If asked to narrow your list to only one name, you might well protest that the task is impossible because each of these people showed a different kind of intelligence. In order to get a little closer to your own definition of intelligence, try the exploration in the box below.

Intelligence is usually defined as an ability to learn from experience. Normally, intelligence is associated with brains, with the ability to make mental associations so that information makes sense. Notice that the very expression—makes sense—suggests a mind-body process rather than a strictly mental one.

As we will learn in the next chapter, people have different styles of learning and perceiving and, therefore, differ in their intelligence. In general, when we consider someone to be intelligent, we observe that person to be

1. capable of organizing abstract ideas to apply to concrete situations,
2. capable of anticipating and predicting causes and effects, and
3. capable of synthesizing information from many sources (Figure 8.1).

With only slight adaptation, these criteria can be applied to the concept of body intelligence. A person who is physically coordinated and responsive is

1. capable of mobilizing appropriate muscles with appropriate force;
2. capable of anticipating or sensing cause and effect; and
3. capable of synthesizing information from many sources, including sensory, emotional, and cultural sources.

---

1. Make a list of five people you know personally whom you consider to be intelligent.

2. Following each name, briefly indicate how his or her intelligence shows. For example:

   My brother—Understands abstract mathematical concepts

   My mother—Has a huge vocabulary, speaks four languages

   Diana—Learns dance steps immediately

3. Finally, think of three examples of your own intelligence.

   I—Am able to plan ahead, can fix my own car, and can survive in the woods

4. How would you define "intelligence"?

**Figure 8.1**

*"How can you think and hit at the same time?"*

—Yogi Berra

Just as a person can memorize a series of mathematical formulas and still not be able to solve a problem, so it is possible for a dancer to memorize a series of steps and still not be able to dance the whole phrase. Without an understanding of the relationships in a math problem, it is difficult to manipulate the figures. Similarly, without a sense of the relationships of the steps in a dance sequence, it is difficult to create a whole that is more than its parts.

## Body Intelligence

A mechanic rebuilding an engine has to know what parts go where as well as how to assemble them correctly. This information can be found in books. Only experience will teach the mechanic just how tight to fit the parts or just how evenly a machine should run. This is analogous to body intelligence. Try this experiment:

Either sitting or standing in a comfortable position, think back to an experience you had that made you very angry. Try to bring the person or people involved clearly into your mind.

Now become aware of any changes that have occurred in your body. Did your jaw clench? Did you find a tightness in your chest? Did your breath become uneven?

Shake off that memory and return to a relaxed, comfortable state. This time think back to an experience you had that brought you great pleasure. Try to bring those circumstances clearly into your mind.

Again, become aware of changes that have occurred in your body. Did you sigh? Did a smile come to your face? Did your chest soften or expand?

Working in the first emotion—anger—produces an outer change in the shape of the body, but that change comes not from trying to look like someone who is angry, but from a muscular recollection of a physical or emotional experience. This is an example of what we will call body intelligence.

The concept of body intelligence goes beyond recall of a particular pattern, skill, or sensation. *Body intelligence* is the ability to coordinate these four components of human action:

## pattern   skill   sensation   emotion

In chapter 1 we discussed the fact that we are always moving and balancing tensions in the body. Those subconscious actions have patterns, require different kinds of skills (such as balancing or tracking tension), are a response to sensation (such as discovery or discomfort), and have an emotional base (such as excitement, impatience, or fear). Consider the response of nail-biting. Let us say that when you become anxious you sometimes bite your nails. A pattern. But a skill? Yes, when you consider that by biting your nails you succeed in displacing your anxiety. Let us say that you also cross your arms over your chest. Another pattern. But a skill? Yes, when you consider that by striking this posture you not only feel safer, but you also communicate to the rest of the world that you feel threatened. Body intelligence is the ability to coordinate pattern, skill, sensation, and emotion into action.

In sports, body intelligence is used by the athlete to achieve a particular goal, such as timing a jump to catch a ball or tucking quickly in a dive. In drama, body intelligence is used by the actor to develop a character. Where does this character carry tension? How does the character stand? Walk? Sit down? Is the character clumsy, nervous, or self-conscious?

In dance, body intelligence is used . . . . How would you finish the sentence? Try this experiment:

Pick a sport. Consider the four components of body intelligence and how they are a part of the sport you chose. For example:

Sport: Soccer

Pattern: Step-step-kick

Skill: Controlling the ball

Sensation: Sensing when to pass, how hard to kick

Emotion: Risk, excitement, competition, danger

Now, what about dance?

Pattern:

Skill:

Sensation:

Emotion:

**Figure 8.2**
How would your life be different if you had this experience as a child?

According to psychologist Howard Gardner, humans have multiple intelligences. In *Frames of Mind*, he lists musical, logical-mathematical, body, and linguistic intelligence as being distinct. As we will see in chapter 9, many factors will contribute to our being good at math, good at languages, or good at sports. There will be differences among those who are envied for being the best in some field. Your basic sports fanatic may be pretty good in all sports, but particularly good at one.

Likewise, all dancers have their strengths based on their own body intelligences. You may be a dancer who quickly perceives a pattern but has difficulty making your body execute that pattern. You may be a dancer who can copy any movement but has a hard time making sense of the sequence. You may be a dancer who enjoys the thrill of leaping and flying but cannot find another speed in yourself to use for slow, sustained movements. Some dancers prefer to be balanced and upright while others prefer to be off-center and unstable. How did these preferences develop? How did you come to sense what feels right for your body (Figure 8.2)?

## Development of Body Intelligence

One of the ongoing debates in developmental psychology concerns nature versus nurture—the debate between those who believe that intelligence is inherited versus those who believe that intelligence is the result of one's environment and circumstances. Which side do you favor?

If we reconsider the three criteria of body intelligence posited earlier in the chapter, a strong case could be made stating that body intelligence is developed from an individual's inherited nature as well as environment. On further investigation, we will also discover that the way a person has adapted to changing physical, mental, and social requirements will have an effect on the evolution of a unique body intelligence.

**Figure 8.3**
Our first dance experiences begin earlier than you might expect.

## Inherited Factors

Even before we are born, we are moving—stretching, kicking, tensing, and reacting to new physical developments (Figure 8.3). Even before arms are fully formed, a fetus pushes and probes at the wall of the womb. By the time an infant arrives in the world and is separated from the mother, the infant is already equipped with patterns and skills, such as grasping and sucking. These and other skills necessary for survival—breathing, swallowing, and communicating—are instinctive.

We arrive in the world with our own genetic coding that will influence our individual development of body intelligence. Although most human survival no longer depends on running, throwing, and digging, our experience of those activities as children does inform us, through body intelligence, about our capabilities as adults. Let us look at some of the genetically determined factors at work and their influence on the development of body intelligence.

### Body Type

People come in all different heights, widths, and weights. The proportions of your body will make some activities easier for you and other activities more difficult. For instance, long legs are an advantage for long-distance runners, but they can be a disadvantage in running sports that require quick changes of direction. The muscle-bound build of a boxer or weight lifter might be a disadvantage in other sports which depend on strength and flexibility.

Your body type is an important, inherited factor that will influence the development of your body intelligence. In general, bodies can be divided into three builds: endomorphic, mesomorphic, and ectomorphic. In fact, very few individuals are true to any one of these classifications. Still, the system of classification is useful for discussing the kinds of activities which are more naturally suitable for one body type or another. These three types are described by William Shelton, Stanley Stevens, and William Tucker in *The Varieties of Human Physique* as follows (see also *The Atlas of Men* by William Shelton).

➡ *Endomorph*—Appears to be round, soft, and weighty. The limbs are short, bones are thick, and the center of gravity is low. The chest and hips are broad, with fatty deposits on the abdomen, chest, arms, and hips. The neck is short, and the head is large. This body is suited for activities in which weight and padding would be advantageous, such as playing contact sports or operating heavy equipment.

➡ *Mesomorph*—Appears to be sturdy, muscular, and rectangular. The bones are thick, the torso is somewhat longer than that of the endomorph, the neck is longer, and the head is smaller. The mesomorph does not carry excess fat in the buttocks and hips. Because this body is endowed with large muscles and evenly proportioned limbs, most physical activities can be accomplished with relative ease and coordination. Of the three body types, mesomorphs are most inclined to regular, rhythmic activities.

➡ *Ectomorph*—Appears to be long, slender, and frail. The bones are small and muscles are thin. The limbs are long, but the torso is short, thus the center of gravity for this body is higher than for others. The ectomorph does not carry fatty tissue and is narrow in the hips and chest. Because of the light body mass, activities which involve air time, such as running, leaping, and diving, are more easily accomplished by this body.

What type of body type describes you most closely? What type of activities are easiest for you?

## Environmental Factors

The person you have become and the person you are in the process of becoming are products of all you have done. Some part of that person developed even before you were able to speak and rationally organize your thoughts. Your early, physical contact with your parents and your siblings had an effect on your feelings about physical contact and your physical sense. How much were you held as an infant? Did your parents comfort you with touch or voice? How were you protected from danger as a child? Were you contained? ("Don't go off the porch!") Restrained? ("Back in the playpen with you!") Were you verbally guided away from hazards? ("Be careful, there's glass over there!") How did you develop the skills to stay alive? How was your physical curiosity encouraged or dampened?

The environments in which you have lived also had an effect on the kind of body intelligence you have developed. People raised in an urban environment will probably carry and conduct themselves differently than those raised in a rural setting. In the United States, east-coast people seem to be different from west-coast people, southerners seem to be different from northerners, and Americans seem to be identifiable all over the world. As a child you were exposed to textures, temperatures, comforts, and dangers that are part of the way you see the world. These variables have influenced your body intelligence—your ability to pattern, to sense, to develop appropriate skills, and respond to your experience (Figure 8.4).

nature vs. nurture

**Figure 8.4**
Many of our adult activities are shaped by our childhood experiences.

## Adaptive Development

The point of this chapter is to provide you with a base of understanding so that you can build on your strengths and positively approach aspects you would like to change.

**Refined motor responses develop in two ways: through imitation and through adaptation.**

We have discussed the instinctive motor responses necessary for survival—swallowing, sucking, breathing—and have mentioned others which usually develop soon after birth—grasping and tracking (that is, following sounds, objects, and possibly scents). We are not given specific instructions in any of these skills, but we come to master them by trial and error, gradually learning to suck and swallow without choking or getting the hiccups, to grasp with appropriate effort, and to follow and even anticipate the origin or path of sights, sounds, and scents. We learn to refine these instinctive motor responses largely through adaptation.

Some adaptations take place as the result of an injury or an illness. Try this experiment in adaptation:

> Pretend that you have twisted your ankle, and walk as if you are favoring that joint. What adaptations do you make to relieve the ankle from bearing weight? Does your opposite arm swing more than it otherwise would? Does your upper body make a circle as you walk? Is there constant tension in the front of your foot? What else do you notice about your adaptations?

If you have been even slightly active in the course of growing up, you have probably suffered slightly from pulled muscles, broken bones, cuts, scrapes, bruises, and combinations of these products of living a little bit dangerously. You have survived, but you may well carry with you scar tissue, weakened limbs, or bad memories—both mental and muscular. Whether you are one of the mind-over-matter types (who claim to be unaffected by pain) or one who gives in completely to any kind of stress, you will still carry the physical memory of the adaptations necessitated by your injury.

Other necessities besides injury and illness will cause an adaptive change in your body intelligence. The necessities of circumstances and customs will furnish you with new patterns and skills to master and new sensory and emotional responses. You walk a little differently when you approach a meeting with someone you deem more powerful than you, do you not? You may wear different clothes to some appointments than you would ordinarily wear—different shoes (that affect your walk), different garments (that affect how you sit or stand). Behaviors that are unacceptable in one circumstance may be expected in another. You adapt. For example, we generally avoid walking or standing close to strangers; however, if you were to move to Tokyo, you would probably become accustomed to this kind of closeness. Your development of refined motor responses—the way you act, react, and move—is partly a product of the circumstances and experiences you have unintentionally encountered.

Your development of refined motor responses is also a product of conscious and sometimes unconscious decisions to mold your behavior—to train, to receive instruction, to model yourself after some ideal. Through instruction by imitation, repetition, and correction you acquire new skills, modify old patterns, and experience new sensations and emotions. Most commonly, we think of training being directed by a teacher or a coach. The example and opinion of these people serve as inspiration to our own development.

When you make a decision to take a dance class or a gymnastics class, you choose to take direction from a teacher when learning to imitate the positions, timing, and basics of the form. When you make a decision to go out for a sport, you put yourself in the hands of the coach who gives you pointers on how to be a better player. But there are other people we use privately to coach our day-to-day activities. Certainly we are coached by our families in the acceptable ways to stand, sit, walk, and respond to others. Our friends coach us in movements, postures, and even personal timing that they find acceptable. Finally, we refine our behavior coached by complete strangers available through the media. Advertisers are grateful for our ready acceptance of these coaches and our eager interest in imitating the models they have designed.

We see, then, that while some aspects of your development of body intelligence come from inherited factors beyond your control, many of the finer points of who you have become come from your environment.

Without a clear recognition of both the goals of your training and your strengths and weaknesses that will make your training *sensible*, your pursuit of imitation can very well be frustrating. It is critical that you learn a process of imitation that enables you to develop in *all* four components of body intelligence—pattern, skill, sensation, and emotion—in order to be able to integrate your mental, physical, and emotional selves.

## Body Intelligence and Dance

The process of dance training can be a tricky balancing act between trying to change the way you are and trying to enjoy the way you are. Dance is a physical activity with physical limits. These limits will vary from dancer to dancer. Your training will involve extending your physical limits—a process that has its rewards and its frustrations. Questions which recur in the training process are: How far am I willing to push my own limits? What am I trying to be like or look like? Why are some movements so difficult and some so easy for me? Why can I remember some steps and not others? The answers to these questions will come from an examination of your body intelligence. Finding the line between straining your physical limits and extending your physical limits, recognizing the difference between affecting someone else's style and absorbing someone else's style, and sensing the difference between duplicating and recreating a sequence of movement are all challenges of dance training.

### Style: Finding the Dance in You

Originally, a *stylus* was a special stick used for making impressions on wax tablets. Today we still use a derivative of the word to describe the kind of impression made on us by another person, place, or thing. For instance, you may describe someone's home as decorated in a modern style—meaning you were impressed with the use of glass, shiny metal, or unconventionally shaped furniture.

You might describe one teacher as having a relaxed style, based on the way you are addressed as students and the kinds of rules you are expected to follow in the class. Another teacher may impress you as having a more conventional style. Remember, style is an instrument used to make an impression. Just as a room can be transformed to a different style, so can a person transform by adopting different styles for different occasions, that is, by selecting different tools, such as choice of words, clothing, posture, or attitude.

When we refer to style in dance we are still talking about the impression a dancer makes with movement. So, where does style come from? In dance, *style* is a product of your efforts and your essence. The style you have as a dancer will come from the physical training you have had and the person you are. Your style will be your integration of the patterns, skills, sensations, and emotions you confront (or invite!) as a dancer. Consider the situations on the next page.

For beginning dancers there is a struggle to simply stand up while also remembering to keep the tummy in, tail down, shoulders dropped, sternum lifted, ribs relaxed, legs straight, and to BREATHE! But eventually, as the sensation of useful alignment becomes second nature and the special demands of your chosen technique (such as a

find the line

1. If asked to create a straight path across your dance space without walking, which would you most likely do?

    a. skip

    b. take giant leaps

    c. crawl

    d. _____

2. The assignment is step-step-(event). Which would you most likely choose?

    a. step-step-turn

    b. step-step-balance

    c. step-step-leap

    d. step-step-_____

Your choice will be conditioned by the space in which you are working. What space did you select from your imagination?

3. Do you generally use your arms when making up movements, or do you "add the arms" once you have gotten the feet organized?

4. When shaping movement, do you work from image (how you look) or from feeling?

5. If someone asked you to demonstrate how you dance, what would you show?

turned-out or parallel base) become more familiar, you will find that you have, in fact, evolved into your own style.

This evolution can easily have both positive and negative aspects. For instance, if you are drawn to the lightness and elegance of ballet, you might approach the tasks in class with an image of yourself floating and balancing easily. This will help. You might also be seduced by tilted heads, spread fingers, and occasionally drooping hands and miss the foundation of these affects. This will not help. All style and no substance.

Perhaps you are drawn to the sensual, beat-driven power of theatrical jazz. The music and the pace appeal to you, and you have a host of popular video, movie, and advertising images to describe not only how you should look but also all the great things that will happen to you once you master that look. Again, the positive and the negative. The good news is that you may discover a new power in your movement style. The bad news is that you may, once again, hit the all-style-no-substance dilemma.

Finally, modern dance may seem to be a good place to discover and to develop your style because you can do anything you want in modern dance, right? Not quite. There is certainly room for personal interpretation and invention in most modern dance techniques, but no technique is without its differentiating substance. Later in this text we will look at some of these differences, but for now our point is that regardless of the technique you study, you will always have two jobs:

1. Discover the essence of the technique.
2. Discover your essence within that technique.

Then you have style.

## Integrity: Finding the Dancer You Are

Your development as a dancer (and as a person) will depend on your integrity. The more you are able to appreciate and work with your unique gifts and talents, the more you will have to offer as a dancer and as a person. If you generally work with outer, other-body goals, your chances of being present for your own transformations are coincidental. Maintaining your integrity, both in classwork and in choreographic work, requires that you continually evaluate how you move and what you are moved by in terms of images, sensations, and motivations. Comparisons and some competition are inevitable in an art form that deals with transforming the same basic material: the human body. Still, you will be ahead of the game if you can use such comparisons to add to your body intelligence.

Chapter 9 discusses differences in perceptual processes and differences in learning styles. Apply that information to identify your own strengths and weaknesses. For instance, rather than pout about how long it takes you to learn a phrase ("Tamisha *always* learns faster than *I* do."), devote your attention to how it is you *do* learn. Do you start with the rhythm of the movement? Do you focus on the big events? Do you work from images?

In this chapter we have discussed differences in the development of body intelligence. How does that information fit in your development as a dancer? It may be true that "*her* legs are so long and thin; *my* legs will never look like that." But unless you are contemplating major surgery, forget her legs. The point is, what about *your* legs?

Your duty as a dancer is to reveal, through the magic of movement, a spark of the soul. Your soul. Your awareness and application of the principles of body intelligence and your dedication to discovering your own unique potential as a dancer will lead you to that magic.

**Think
About
It**

1. Describe the difference between personality and style. (Is the way André appears the way that he really is?)

2. Consider ways that you deliberately adopt a style that is different from your regular nature. What are the circumstances that lead you to this? Analyze this adopted behavior in terms of the four components of body intelligence.

   a. What is the pattern? (shuffling my feet)

   b. What is the skill? (successfully imitating the walk of a laid-back rock star)

   c. What is the sensation? (comfortable for a little while, then my neck starts to hurt)

   d. What is the emotion? (When I walk like this person I feel more acceptable and more comfortable socially.)

3. Early in this chapter you saw a quote from one of the most important men in baseball history. What did Yogi Berra mean when he asked, "How can you think and hit at the same time?" What does this have to do with dance?

4. If you were a tree, what kind of tree would you be? If you were an animal, what kind of animal would you be? How do each of these choices reflect your body intelligence?

5. What is the earliest dance combination you can remember learning? (This may be from this year's class or from an earlier time in your life.) How well can you repeat the combination today? Polish that performance and identify three adjectives that you associate with the memory (such as cute, nervous, or petrified).

6. Develop a short movement phrase (eight counts should be sufficient). Perform the phrase in the style of the person you think is the best dancer in your class. Perform the phrase in the style of a person in your family. Perform the phrase as an audition. Perform the phrase as a gift.

# 9

# Modes of Perception

The *way* we perceive shapes *what* we perceive. By looking at how you receive, store, and retrieve information, you can consider how your own brain might work, how your feelings might be developed, and why you see the world as you do. This kind of self-awareness may be generally valuable, but it is of particular interest to those of us involved in developing our creative resources.

In this chapter we will look at the senses we use to perceive the world around us. We will look at the ways we process those perceptions, that is, what we do with the sensory information that comes to us. These investigations will involve looking at differences between perceiving and imagining, between physical and mental processes of perceiving, and between processing information using your right brain and your left brain. Most people have a dominant system for collecting information. People tend to favor one of three modes of perception and learn best by seeing, hearing, or physically manipulating their environment. This chapter's title summarizes the topic that could also be called "How you come to know what you know." In each chapter we have identified natural talents and ways to develop new skills that enable you to be a more competent creator and communicator, not just in dance but in other aspects of your life. In this chapter we will continue to focus on ways to help you increase your awareness of the world and your understanding of what you have to offer based on what you perceive.

Whether you become a dancer, painter, actor, writer, sculptor, or musician, you will be involved in translating or creating human experiences into particularly sensual experiences. But if you think about it, whether or not you specialize in the arts, you will still benefit from understanding and expanding your own perceptive and creative processes. How does a parent use these skills? How does an athlete apply the perceptive and creative processes to training? How would this kind of awareness benefit you as a student?

## What Are the Senses?

Most people would not know what to say if you asked them to list their "modalities of sensibility." So you would clarify: "Your senses; what are the senses you use to collect information about the world?" Ah! This is more familiar. Most would answer sight, sound, taste, touch, and smell, and they would be right. Basically. These are the standard five senses that first come to mind, but there are others that are especially important for those who study movement and the perception of movement.

Modern theorists contend that there are as many as *41* different modes of sensing. Think of these as 41 different trains coming into one station. Clearly, most passengers are on 5 of those trains (the five standard senses), but the other 36 have a purpose, too. For our purposes we will focus on the following eight senses:

- ➥ Vision
- ➥ Hearing
- ➥ Touch
- ➥ Taste
- ➥ Smell
- ➥ Vestibular sense (sense of balance)
- ➥ Kinesthetic (muscle sense)
- ➥ Organic sense (internal pain or comfort)

Of all the senses, vision and hearing have received the most research attention, perhaps because these are the two modalities which we humans use most to perceive the world. When describing a person, for instance, we rarely describe how that person smells, stands, or walks; we usually begin with hair color and style, height, weight, and possibly age and race. For most people, vision is the primary sense.

Pick up this book, and make a mental note of all the senses you are using while holding this book and reading from it. Now, as you set this book down, close your eyes, and take a moment to be aware of all the other senses you are using right now—the sounds in your reading area, the light, the comfort of the furniture, the smells, and the taste you have in your mouth.

What other thoughts came to you as you focused on each sense?

## Vision

The process of vision has been studied extensively. We know, for instance, that the image we see—the image that comes through the pupil of the eye—appears on the retina upside down, but the visual information is stored as a right-side-up image in the brain. We know that each eye sends its own image to the brain where one image is created. Basically, we know that the eye and the brain interact to make sense of what is seen.

As dancers, vision is obviously a very important sense. A performance is a visual event. A dance happens, as we discussed in part II, in space, time, and with energy. Is it possible to perform a dance on the radio? Vision is also critical when studying dance technique. Much of dance training involves imitating what you see the teacher demonstrate. This method of training is particularly Western, however. For instance, in traditional Balinese dance training, the teacher stands *behind* the student and physically molds the student's movement patterns.

For some people it would be inconceivable that one could learn to dance without being able to imitate movement, yet others find imitation a frustrating way to begin learning. Can you think of two ways that your sense of vision helps your dancing? Now can you think of two ways your sense of vision interferes with your dancing?

## Hearing

The process of hearing is also well understood. Essentially, sound waves are received by the eardrum, which vibrates differently according to how loud, soft, high, or low the sound is. Dogs are capable of interpreting very high pitches—sounds which are out of the range of normal human hearing. Elephant trainers have noted that although they cannot actually *hear* a sound, their bodies often vibrate in the presence of their elephants who, they suspect, are communicating with sounds which are below the range of normal human hearing. Although we humans may not be as sensitive to vibrations as other creatures, we are, nevertheless, able to interpret vibrations or sounds to identify familiar and unfamiliar people, places, and things. As with the process of seeing, the brain and the ear interact to make sense of what is heard.

Most dance is accompanied by sound, whether it is produced by a grand orchestra or a solo thumb-piano. Some dances, tap dance, for instance, produce sound as part of the dance. Even dances done in silence make us aware of sound or the lack of sound. Hearing is another important sense for a dancer's awareness. When developing your awareness of your hearing sense, remember that there are many possibilities for accompaniment other than what we commonly call music. Sounds from nature, machines, humans, conversations, poetry, work, play, distortion, and synthesizers can all make interesting backgrounds for dance.

When the audience is able to hear heavy landings or clunking shoes during a dance style in which the dancer is meant to appear weightless or ethereal, the magic is ruined. But in many dance styles, the sound created when the body contacts the ground is an exciting element to cultivate.

## Taste and Smell

Taste and smell are closely related senses. Both processes send signals to the brain on the same pathway. It is known that there are four taste sensations: sweet, sour, bitter, and salty. It is also known that different parts of the tongue are sensitive to these sensations. You are probably aware of the relationship of taste and smell if you have noticed how a head cold changes the way food tastes. Similarly, if you are distracted by a foul smell, you may notice it is difficult to enjoy the taste of even your favorite food. Scientists say that we are capable of distinguishing between six smells: flowery, fruity, rotten, resinous, spicy, and burned (J.G. Beebe-Center, "Standards for the use of the gusto scale," *Journal of Psychology*, vol. 28, 1949). While the manufacturers of deodorants and perfumes would like us to believe that our lives depended on smell, the fact is that humans do not regularly rely on smell and taste for survival.

As dancers, how can we apply our awareness of these two senses to our art? What kind of dance could be made by you and three friends if you each became one of the four taste sensations? Which one would you be?

## Touch

*Touch* is the common term for what science now refers to as the *cutaneous sense* or skin sense. Presumably, the title has been modified to include sensations received by the surface of the skin, as opposed to sensations received at one touchpoint. In any case, the cutaneous sense is the sense you use to detect temperature, pressure, and texture (Figure 9.1).

In dance, we hold, catch, push, pull, and support each other. In some dance forms, such as ballroom dance, the partners communicate their directions with subtle pressures. Contact improvisation is a modern dance form that is based almost

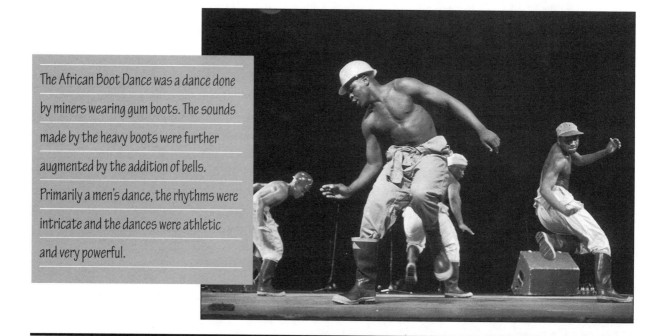

The African Boot Dance was a dance done by miners wearing gum boots. The sounds made by the heavy boots were further augmented by the addition of bells. Primarily a men's dance, the rhythms were intricate and the dances were athletic and very powerful.

**Figure 9.1**

The brush of fabric, the rush of a breeze are simple delights experienced through the cutaneous sense.

completely on touch. Dance sequences are not set in this form; they occur spontaneously as the dancers contact each other with different parts of their bodies.

Groups of dancers regularly use the cutaneous sense in their performances. To understand how, try this experiment with a friend:

> Close your eyes and stand very still. Ask your friend to hold a hand up close to, but not touching, your face. See if you are able to tell when your friend's hand is there and when it is not. Are there other parts of your body that can feel this presence?
>
> Plug your ears and close your eyes so that you can neither see nor hear your friend moving. Say "Stop," and see if you can point to where your friend is standing.

Dancers need to be able to sense each other without seeing or speaking. To do this they use their sense of hearing, but they also depend heavily on the cutaneous sense.

## Organic Sense

The cutaneous sense informs the body about pleasurable and dangerous sensations—for instance, the difference between light scratching and scratching which draws blood. The cutaneous sense monitors sensations on the surface of the body. There is another sense which informs the brain about the state of affairs within the body—the organic sense. If you eat too much, the pressure from your bloated tummy sends a message to your brain that it is time to lie down and take some time for digestion. If you are ill and run a fever, the message goes to your brain to slow the system down for healing. It is more than just a chemical reaction; this is the sense that warns you that your body will suffer if you continue *before* you have eaten too much, stayed up too late, or read too long in low light.

Dancers are notoriously insensitive to their organic sense. Because dancing can be so physically demanding, dancers often ignore the messages from the organic sense to eat, rest, and stop certain activities. The results of ignoring one's organic sense can easily be injury, pain, fatigue, and illness. A healthy respect for the wisdom of the body will lead to a longer and healthier dance life.

## Vestibular Sense

A vestibule is a small room, a hall, or a passage that you have to go through on your way into a house or building. The *vestibular sense* can be said to be the sense that balances the outside with the inside experience. Through a fluid mechanism in the inner ear, you automatically adjust yourself to stay balanced and upright. This is the sense that you automatically use for orientation, that keeps you from walking into the wall when you are aiming for the door, and that helps you pin the tail close to the donkey—not on the floor—when playing the party game. Without your vestibular sense you would not know the difference between the floor and the wall after being spun around blindfolded. If you spin too much, you will become disoriented and unbalanced. Have you ever experienced motion sickness? In this case your vestibular sense overreacts and sends a message to the brain saying your body is being asked to adjust to abnormal pressure changes. This message will in turn trigger the organic sense—the internal sense that warns the brain of danger.

## Kinesthetic Sense

The *kinesthetic sense* is the muscle sense. To understand this sense better, try these three experiments:

1. While looking straight ahead, take your right hand behind you, and try to grab your left foot. You may lift your left foot up to meet your hand.
2. Hold your arms straight in front of your body, about shoulder-width apart. With your eyes closed, try to touch the tips of your little fingers together.
3. Repeat the second experiment, but this time start with your little fingers and go through all five digits, noting two things: Are some fingers easier to match? Are you able to perform this task more quickly with practice (even though you cannot see what you are doing)?

The kinesthetic sense is very important not only to dancers but to all humans. Without a kinesthetic—muscle—sense you would not be able to coordinate the tasks in the experiments above. Your movements would be jerky, and your reactions would tend to be uncoordinated. *Kinesis* is Greek for "motion"; the kinesthetic sense is the one you use to control your motion—your muscles. In other words, you probably executed the first experiment above without falling over backward. Why? Because your kinesthetic sense enabled you to counterbalance while leaning backward to grab your foot.

In the second experiment, you may well have brought your hands together quickly and then carefully closed the last few inches. You may have been initially unsuccessful at touching just the fingertips, but chances are, with very short practice, your kinesthetic sense about the task had developed quickly, and you were able to complete the task blindly and quickly.

The kinesthetic sense informs the brain about the amount of effort the body needs to expend, the kind of effort (burst of energy, a long, slow haul, and so on), and the muscles which will be required for a task. The kinesthetic sense informs the brain about space, depth, surface, resistance, and the muscular reaction which will be appropriate. The kinesthetic sense informs the brain and body about time, such as for relaxing, fighting, or retreating from a situation.

The kinesthetic sense is critical to dance because it is, essentially, a muscular translation of experience. As we shall see in the next section, no sense is truly independent of any of the other senses. But, as we shall also learn, while we all see, hear, smell, taste, touch, feel, and move, we do have individual preferences in the ways that we draw on our senses.

## The Interrelationship of the Senses

Although we may debate some ways of classifying the senses, we can agree that the senses are how we acquire information about our world. We organize and classify our experiences using our senses in combination. If you were to blindfold yourself, open the refrigerator, and get out a bottle, you might not know exactly what was in the bottle you were holding, but you would know that you were not holding a cucumber or an apple. Even with your eyes covered, you could visualize the shape of the bottle and what the label might look like. Having decided you are probably holding a bottle of cola, you take the top off and have a sniff. Whoa! This smells like . . . like . . . could it be *tomato*? You listen to the bottle and hear it fizzing like a soda. But you have never heard of tomato soda. You decide not to drink until you have more information. You remove the blindfold, and what do you see?

Really. How did you respond to tomato soda? Did you imagine the taste, the look of the bottle, the look of the liquid, or some other aspect related to tomato soda? In your own way, you took what you know about soda, what you know about tomatoes, and combined the two ideas. Maybe such a thing as tomato soda exists. If you saw a bottle with a tomato-soda label on a shelf in a store, you would go through a similar imaginative process to decide whether you would like to buy it and try it. Based on your experience with both soda and tomatoes, you would, however, know that this was not a product to take home and pour on the furniture to help protect the finish. Even if you knew nothing about furniture care, your senses would probably inform you that neither soda nor tomatoes would make furniture shiny.

*use your imagination*

Through our senses and our sense memory we perceive the world. To perceive is to recognize based on experience. A key thought: *based on experience*. We each perceive the world according to our unique backgrounds. Someone from a rural environment may recognize different smells than someone from an urban environment. Someone who comes from one region of the country may have difficulty understanding someone who comes from another area. Any two people will probably have different interpretations of a painting, sculpture, or piece of music. They may appreciate different aspects of the same dance.

Now look at Figure 9.2, and describe what you see. Be inventive. What country might this be? Why is this little girl wearing white in the midst of all that construction and dirt? Where might she be going? Why might others not find her dress unusual? In fact, this photo was taken in a predominantly Latin section of Manhattan just a few years ago. The religion in this area was predominantly Catholic. If you are familiar with the culture of Catholicism, you might come to a different conclusion about why the young girl in the picture is dressed in white and why no one in the street finds her unusual.

Imagine you are standing on that street in Manhattan. Describe what you imagine you would perceive if you were standing where this picture was taken. Do not limit yourself to exactly what is in this picture—use your imagination. Is someone calling that girl's name? Can you smell something cooking? Is there a dry taste in your mouth? Are you hot or cold?

**Figure 9.2**

What do you see?

In every living moment, your brain is processing sensory information about your experience. Your senses work together to provide that information, identifying, sorting, and probing new input. Some senses work automatically, some senses are developed quite consciously, but in all, your perceptions, intuitions, and reactions are the product of the interrelationship of your senses.

The experiments above required you to use your imagination more than your actual perceptions, but by reviewing your responses you may observe something about your *perceptual preferences*, or the senses that make the most sense to you. Did you find it easiest to add visual details to your descriptions, or was it easier for you to imagine the sounds or the smells in your descriptions? Was the whole process of imagining difficult or easy for you? Did you enjoy using your imagination, or do you find such experiments frustrating?

Perception is a very interesting process involving a person's mental, physical, and emotional reactions to the environment. In *Theories of Perception*, F. Allport listed 13 ways to explain this process of learning, storing, and retrieving information about our experiences. There have been even more theories proposed in the years since his book was published in 1955. For our purposes we do not need to go into detailed descriptions of all these theories. What is interesting is the fact that there are so many different ways of explaining how we learn, store, and react to the objects, people, and situations in our lives. The process is still something of a mystery. What keeps it mysterious is the fact that no two people's experiences of anything will be exactly the same; in fact, as we grow and learn, *our* perceptions change based on our experience.

Notice, in the examples above, that you were not asked what one sense informed you about these activities; you were asked what sense*s*. Your senses work together to compile information. One sense will trigger another. Can you think of a smell that would trigger a visual sense? How about the smell of your favorite food? And speaking of food, can you think of a sound that would trigger your sense of taste? How about the sound of biting into an apple? Can you think of a sound that would trigger a muscle reaction? How about the sound of nails on the blackboard? Or the sound of squealing tires? Or even the sound of a baby crying?

For any of these examples you may well have found other senses being aroused. Thinking of the sound of nails on the blackboard may have brought to your mind a particular classroom or even a specific day in your life. The suggestion of your favorite food may have left your mouth watering. The senses work together in conscious and unconscious ways. Try this experiment:

> Choose three senses. Write them down.
>
> Write down one pleasant and one unpleasant experience you imagine or have had through that sense.
>
> Now go back through these pleasant and unpleasant sense memories, and think of them in terms of the other senses. Consider the ways the senses work together.

## Perceptual Processes

When we perceive we receive information through our senses, and we create our own way of looking at the world. What does it mean when we say that we are the sum total of our experience?

If you have had some good experiences with mathematical challenges, you may approach other math problems with confidence based on your experience. If you have been less than successful with problems of this sort, you may find yourself shutting off when math skills are required. If you have had good experiences with language problems—you remember vocabulary easily, you express yourself easily—you will approach challenges involving language with confidence. But you may be someone who makes a lot of mistakes in spoken or written work. Why do you think you might be strong in some areas but weak in others? Positive and negative experiences clearly play a part, but it may help us to consider how these self-images develop.

Sometimes we are aware of positive or negative experiences that have opened or closed our perceptions, and sometimes we are not. A young child may have heard herself described many times as very shy and may, therefore, have adopted that description, never challenging and, in fact, reinforcing that perception. One negative experience with swimming may shut down another child's interest in water if he is never encouraged to expand on that first negative experience. Many American children do not like mushrooms. The texture and even the name seem to have unpleasant associations. As adults, many pay dearly for these once-dreaded morsels. How *do* we develop these preferences, these associations, and these perceptions about the world and about ourselves? It may help to consider how your own brain processes your experiences.

### How Does the Brain Work?

The first thing we need to say is that if we knew exactly how the human brain works, the world would be a different place. The mystery of the human brain is the mystery of the human race. Theories and studies abound, but no one theory or study offers a complete explanation which includes chemical, behavioral, and spiritual aspects of perceptual processing. However, we do not need to wait for the perfect theory to understand something about the way the brain works. We simply need to be aware that no theory is yet complete and let our own curiosity add to current theory.

One such theory is that the brain is divided into two sides, or hemispheres. There has been considerable research on how these two sides work together as well as investigation on what information gets stored where. Although each of our senses has its special spot in the brain, as we have demonstrated in the preceding experiments, no sense is triggered independent of the other senses. Therefore, the way we *process* information is closely tied to the way we perceive. The two hemispheres of the brain handle information differently.

According to this theory, the left hemisphere processes information in a linear fashion. This method of processing means that you interpret information according

*We are the sum total of our experience.*

to what comes next, what rules apply, and what parts are involved, instead of processing information in terms of relationships, the tendency of the right hemisphere. Left-brain functions are described as sequential, logical, and mathematical; right-brain functions are thought of as holistic, pattern-creating, musical, and spatial.

### Test yourself.
### True or False: 3 is half of 8.

Well, if you apply mathematical rules of division, or left-brain reasoning, your answer would be "False"; however, if you look at the pattern that the number makes and slice it in two, then, yes, the pattern of the 3 resembles the right side of the pattern of the 8. That would be right-brain processing. Look at the following patterns from *The Two Sided Mind* by L.V. Williams and find the element which breaks the pattern:

### A B C D E F C G H I J K
### O * O * O O * O * O * O

Did you do this task by moving your eyes from left to right, checking each item in order until you found the one that did not fit? Then you used sequential processing. Or did you look at the whole line and let your eyes focus on the item that broke the pattern? That is simultaneous processing.

Williams calls the right-brain process "simultaneous processing"; the person is inclined to look at the whole in order to understand its parts (page 26). A left-brain process would look at the individual parts to understand the whole. Do you know what process you prefer?

The quiz on page 128 may indicate if you are more inclined to use your left brain, your right brain, or if you operate equally out of both.

Obviously, it would not be reasonable to assume that a simple five-question test could offer conclusive proof about whether a person tends to operate from the left or the right brain, but you may have a better idea about the differences in left-brain and right-brain preferences.

For instance, the first two questions have to do with which side of the brain you are apt to use to visualize or to do computation. Because the right brain controls the left side of the body, glancing to the left would indicate that the right brain is being used. As we said above, the right brain normally processes spatial, relational, musical, and imaginary things. The left brain usually processes logical, verbal, sequential, and rational things. You may well have used your left brain to answer the second question.

Consider your responses to the last three questions. Knowing what you now know about the characteristics of a right- or left-dominant person, where do you see yourself?

1. Can you remember where you sat in your fourth-grade classroom? When you recalled that scene, did your eyes move

      a. to the right

      b. to the left

      c. stay in the center

2. When asked to multiply 36 by 15 in your head, do your eyes move

      a. to the left

      b. to the right

      c. in the center

3. Are you

      a. more of a day person

      b. more of a night person

      c. both equally

4. From the following list of words, check *five* that best describe you:

| | | | |
|---|---|---|---|
| _____ a. | Analytical | _____ k. | Verbal |
| _____ b. | Logical | _____ l. | Able to grasp "wholes" |
| _____ c. | Musical | _____ m. | Dominant |
| _____ d. | Mathematical | _____ n. | Intellectual |
| _____ e. | Artistic | _____ o. | Able to synthesize |
| _____ f. | Innovative | _____ p. | Spatially oriented |
| _____ g. | Intuitive | _____ q. | Linearly oriented |
| _____ h. | Self-controlled | _____ r. | A reader |
| _____ i. | Detail-minded | _____ s. | A synthesizer |
| _____ j. | Emotional | _____ t. | Able to use analogies |

5. My best ideas most often come to me

      a. just as I am waking up

      b. when I have a deadline to meet

      c. when I have finished my research on a topic

## Hemispheric Dominance and Dance

You may find this information about the brain interesting, but what does it have to do with dance? Here are a few questions which may lead us to answers:

1. Think back to a dance you remember seeing. Were you impressed with the sequence of steps, the beauty of the performers, or the feeling the dance aroused in you?

2. Think back to a dance you remember making yourself. Did you have a specific message to relate? Were you dancing as yourself or as some other character? Was the feeling you held as a performer the same or different from the feeling you hoped to express?

3. Think back to a conversation about a dance that you have had with your friends or classmates. How is the work evaluated? Does everyone agree on what worked and what did not?

There is one important point to be made with regard to hemispheric dominance and dance. Dance is basically a right-brain activity. It is spatial, relational, and not particularly logical. Some of the most frequent responses to dance performances are, "Weird," or "I didn't *get* it." There most certainly is a delicate balance between giving an audience meaningful clues about your choreographic intent and beating them over the head with your personal, choreographic truth. Bearing in mind that, according to the two-hemisphere theory, we are a left-brain culture, we must work both as artists and as audience to discover and develop our right-brain selves.

## Modes of Perception

Along with the recent interest in left- versus right-brain processing, educators are investigating the differences people have in their *modes of perception*. To understand this better, consider the situations in the questions on page 130.

These questions all pertain to your preferred mode of perception. There are three modes, or ways, of perceiving:

1. Visual mode
2. Hearing mode
3. Kinesthetic mode

Most of us can operate out of all three modes, but our strengths may be particularly in one or two. A person who is most comfortable with the visual mode will probably look closely at an infant in a crib, make eye contact, and watch the way the child moves and wiggles. A person who is most comfortable with the hearing mode would be more inclined to make noises to the child and would be delighted if the child made noises back. Finally, the kinesthetically oriented person would probably touch the child's

1. When introduced to an infant, do you

    a. talk to the child

    b. look closely at the child

    c. touch the child

2. Which of these situations would bother you the most?

    a. clutter on the floor of a room

    b. sand in your bed

    c. distracting conversations

3. When you have to remember a phone number do you

    a. write it down

    b. repeat it to yourself

    c. remember it by listening to it

4. When you recognize a relative stranger, what are you most likely to recognize?

    a. the person's face

    b. the person's name

    c. some specific aspect (mannerism, walk, etc.)

hands, try to get the child to hold hands, or simply extend the arms to take the child to hold.

The responses to the other questions roughly indicate the following preferences:

| 2. Visual | 3. Visual | 4. Visual |
|-----------|-----------|-----------|
| Kinesthetic | Kinesthetic | Hearing |
| Hearing | Hearing | Kinesthetic |

Again, you may have found that you used all three modes to answer the above questions. These questions are by no means conclusive. We all operate in these different modes at different times. As a student, you may find an awareness of your mode preferences to be very useful. Suppose your teacher spends most of the class lecturing and writing on the board. That will work well for you if you are a hearing-mode person. But if you learn best by repeating or by writing things out yourself, you are going to be in trouble.

## Modes of Perception and Dance

Why might modes of perception be a topic relevant to dancers?

In the same way that this awareness can benefit you in your other classes, an awareness of your modes of perception can benefit you as a dancer, as a student of dance, as a choreographer, and as an audience member.

As a dancer you are physically inclined—you find it easy or, at least, intriguing—to use your body expressively. There may be some kinds of expression which come naturally to you, such as strong, bold movements or soft, subtle movements. You may be particularly aware of strong, bold shapes in your world or strong, bold people in your life, and you may have developed a patterned response. By continuing to develop your kinesthetic awareness, you open a world of possibilities for expression.

As a student of dance you are often asked to repeat a movement pattern or exercise which has just been demonstrated. By relying on all three modes, you increase your chances of being able to perform the movement. You may ask yourself, "How does it sound?" You might visualize a group of tense muscles relaxing. By working from your kinesthetic mode and expanding into other ways of perceiving, you will increase the strategies available to you to meet the task.

As a choreographer you can expand your inventive capacities by drawing on all three modes. Watch other people, imitate the motions of nonhuman things, and use your body to make sounds visible. Any choreographer can get stuck in a rut of familiar movement, but by being aware of your modes of perception, you may be able to switch modes and discover new expressions.

## Perceiving and Creating

We are the sum of our experiences. Our individual perceptions do affect the creative process. Later in this text we will return to the subject of the creative process as it applies directly to choreography. If we recall that choreography is the design of movement for its own sake, we can begin to apply what we know about perception to the simplest choreographic choices. We can apply these principles of perception to other classwork and to developing all our creative resources.

**Think About It**

1. Now that you have had a chance to consider the three modes of perception, apply what you know to the next performance you see by looking for clues as to what was the choreographer's dominant mode of perception. Does the work appear to be most heavily directed by the music? Does the work appear to be designed from the outside to the inside (which would suggest that the choreographer was working from a visual mode) or does the work have a strong organic feel (which would suggest that the choreographer was working from a kinesthetic mode)? What role does your dominant mode of perception play in the way you perceive dance?

2. One of the main goals of this chapter is to increase your sensitivity to and your awareness of the world through which you move so that you are in a better position to use your daily experiences as resources for your dance work. Without actually creating or choreographing the dances, make a list of the eight senses, and pair each with the seed of an idea for a dance that could be based on that sense. For instance:

*Vision*—Make fluorescent-colored sticks that are the same length as the bones of the arms and legs. Tape these sticks to a dark leotard. Experiment with the shapes these make in black light. Make a dance. (This is a variation on an idea developed by Oskar Schlemmer, a Bauhaus designer in the 1920s.)

*Hearing*—Choreograph a dance to a familiar piece of classical music, and perform the piece in a space where the audience can only hear short measures of the music. Or, perform it where the audience is outside watching the dance through windows and cannot hear the music at all. Or, let the dancers listen to the music on headsets, and play different music for the audience to hear.

3. There is a fun children's game called "Treasure Tray" that is a memory-teaser played by placing assorted unrelated items on a tray, showing the tray for a brief period, and asking all the players to write down the names of as many items as they can remember. As a more mature variation on this game, try showing a short movement sequence to a group of friends, and see how much of your sequence can be imitated and how accurately this can be done. Experiment with including strong cues useful to hearing-dominant learners and strong cues for kinesthetic-dominant learners. Experiment with asking respondents to close their eyes and reiterate a dance they could only hear being made.

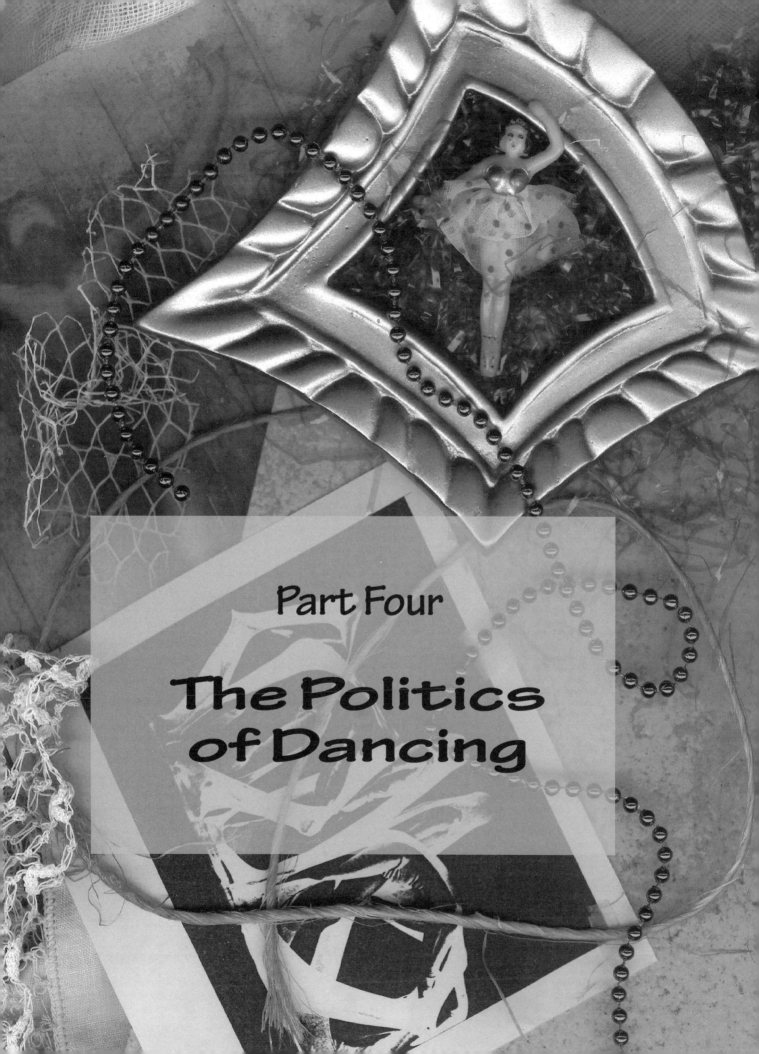

# Part Four

# The Politics of Dancing

# Making a Statement Through Dance

**W**e have examined the characteristics of dance, studied the elements of the art form, and considered ways that an individual's physical and perceptual strengths will influence dance and choreographic choices. We are now prepared to integrate all of this information as we consider how one goes about using dance to make a statement about the world and one's experience of the world.

This text aims to enable you to access your unique brand of creativity and, using the art of dance, share some aspect of yourself with others. Ideally, this involves finding a way (or several ways) to integrate the physical, emotional, and spiritual aspects of yourself. When you can find this integration, chances are you have created something original.

In this chapter we will focus on two things:

1. How to have an original thought
2. How to explore your original thought

You will find this chapter useful both in your dance class and in other activities that require you to think for yourself and to be creative. Different activities require creative, problem-solving strategies, and it is usually safe to assume that there are at least two ways to solve any problem—most of the time there are even more. This kind of thinking will be central to our approach to making a statement using dance. We will assume that there are as many dance solutions as there are choreographers, and each choreographer will bring wisdom and experience to the dance creation.

## "Movement Resources I Have Known"

Whether you have been asked to construct a short sequence or an evening-length work, at this point in your dance career you have probably had a chance to try your hand at some choreographic enterprise. Recall some of the resources you may have used to form your studies or dances. For the purposes of this text, study will refer to a short dance—complete with beginning, middle, and end—that presents an in-depth investigation of the movement possibilities of a narrowly defined topic. For instance, a study on rising and falling might include 20 ways to rise and fall. In the course of finding those ways, you might discover a dance about life and death, a dance about success and failure, or a dance about some other contrast. Your rising and falling dance would still be considered a study—a string of movement options. A study is to a dance what a sketch is to a painting.

When you are asked to create a dance study, a sketch, a scientific abstract, or a synopsis of a play, you will go through the same creative process of identifying all the resources available to you that might help you put your own ideas into perspective. In the composition work you have done to this point, you have drawn on a number of resources which you may or may not have consciously considered.

### Technique

Not all composition classes include the study of a particular dance style or technique. If imitation has been a part of your training, you will be likely to incorporate the movement skills that interest you as you continue to explore your newly developing physical skills. If imitation has not been stressed in your training, you will draw on styles of movement that you find familiar, comfortable, and acceptable. These are your techniques.

Regardless of which techniques you have been exposed to, you have, no doubt, found certain moves which just feel good to you. You may have discovered a new height to your leaps, a new way to go to the floor, a new strength in some part of your body that enables you to do other movements new to you. Exercises and combinations learned in your technique classes can be a good starting point for dance studies, particularly if you work with material that you enjoy doing and feel you do well.

Suppose you are blessed with long hamstrings (the common name for the collection of gluteal muscles which extend the leg from the hip joint). Length and flexibility in these muscles make it relatively easy for you to do certain movements, such as high kicks and splits. Chances are your studies will have a lot of high kicks and a split or two—movements which are impressive, extraordinary, and happen to be easy for you to do. Recall from chapter 1 that one of the criteria that distinguishes dance from other physical activities is that dance incorporates extraordinary movements. Without much physical or creative effort, you can whip out movements that are going to pass as dance and will be impressive. This is not to imply that there is anything wrong with using your natural talents. In fact, quite the contrary; it is a good idea to work with your unique gifts and talents. Beware, however, of getting stuck in the habits of easy solutions. Sure, it is a pleasure to watch people move with confidence, but it can get boring quickly if a dancer can only do one thing, such as turn, do high kicks, or hold a leg extended. As you sample and draw from your techniques, bear in mind that as exciting as it is to see a dancer move with confidence, it is also exciting to see a person take risks.

As you apply the principles of technique in your composition work, be aware that technique is a beginning, a resource, a base. Technique does not speak. *You*, through your unique way of using technique, deliver the statement.

## Media

As we discussed in previous chapters on perception and body intelligence, you are all that you have seen, heard, felt, smelled, tasted, and sensed.

The media have certainly tried to be a part of those experiences. Is television part of your life? Do you read the newspaper? Do you look through magazines? Do you listen to the radio or to recorded music? All of these resources—deliberate or otherwise—inform your dance studies.

New fashions in posture, dress, language, music, and recreation continually replace those that were once unacceptable; they suddenly become the new standard of acceptability. In general, what is familiar is what is acceptable. You and your classmates may have a familiar way of moving to your favorite songs. Images in magazines, on billboards, and on packages will reinforce a way of dressing, standing, walking, and relaxing. These are resources you use in creating your own compositions. Advertisers hope that these will be your standards of beauty, tension, and expression. Perhaps you have accepted these standards. Perhaps you have established your own.

Your standards will provide you with a sense of what is good, interesting, funny, or inspiring. As discussed in the section on technique, it can be a pleasure to watch a dancer move with confidence. Even if we have seen similar movements before, we will enjoy seeing them again if the dancer presents them with new life. Likewise, if you can breathe new life into movement patterns that have become clichés, you can use the resources of the media in a creative, innovative way.

You can use a test—the "That's stupid!" test—to determine if you are locked into clichéd standards. Often, "That's stupid!" is a way of saying, "That's different from what I'm familiar with." As you are able to appreciate different kinds of expression, the quick dismissal will give way to more specific observations.

Remember this test as you examine media resources for new dance patterns. Some sources that may already have been useful to you are movies and videos about dance history. Often these are the most direct sources available for understanding dances from other cultures. Through these resources we can see that many of the conventions we may associate with contemporary dance did not apply to dance in earlier days. For instance, men used to be much more involved with dance than has been the case in modern Western culture. Consider, as well, that today's image of a ballerina is of a very

*create your own compositions*

thin, long-legged woman. But in the early days of ballet, ballerinas were not nearly as thin as they are required to be today. Likewise, modern dancers were strong and tended to be more stout; however, contemporary professional modern dancers tend to resemble the traditional ballerina image. Times change. The resources of the media can open our eyes to the possibilities of what has been and also give us a way to look objectively at what is.

When using the media as a resource for original thought, bear in mind that in this art form an original thought involves the integration of mind, body, and soul. Sure! Steal the moves that appeal to you from a commercial or a program, but take care to invest your own mind, body, and soul as you work with and recreate this material.

## Other Students

Another great movement resource you may have used in your dance compositions is the talent of your peers. As you have no doubt discovered, working with other people has advantages and disadvantages. Different choreographers work with the movement resources of other dancers in different ways. As a dancer you will soon discover that you feel more comfortable working with certain kinds of processes more than others. When you are wearing the choreographer's hat, it can be helpful to maintain some perspective on the expectations you have of the dancers working with you. Consider a few of the more common categories into which choreographers can often be classified.

### The Dictator

You will find some choreographers who simply relish the opportunity to be in charge and have their ideas heard. It can seem that the opportunity to direct is as or more important than the opportunity to create. On the bright side, this kind of choreographer has a clear vision of the way things should be. This person is not usually interested in entertaining other people's ideas, so this means that the rehearsal process does not involve a lot of discussion and democratic weighing of options. It also means that if you as a dancer do not think much of the choreography, you keep your ideas to yourself and find a way to do what is asked. The dictator choreographer is a good person to work with if you enjoy being directed and molded. This choreographer can help you to discover new options that you would probably not have chosen if you were working on your own. This is not a good person to work with if you enjoy having input in the creative process.

### The Visionary

You will find that there are choreographers who require seemingly impossible tasks in the name of art. They can see the dance in their heads and can recognize opportunities for stunning and spectacular human feats as they direct their dancers. In general, these choreographers do take into account the skills of the individual dancer and always keep one eye open for idiosyncrasies that could be transformed into spectacle or special effect. They will ask for the impossible, and they will often get it! These are choreographers who forget that the human body is governed by the laws of gravity and energy, and they push those laws to the limits. They are great people to work with if you are the sort of person who enjoys taking risks and enjoys being pushed to explore the outer limits of your endurance, balance, and flexibility. This can be exhilarating!

## The Sponge

Some choreographers use dancers as if they were puddles of ideas waiting to be mopped up and put in a glass. With a few vague ideas, they begin with a "Try this, no this, no this . . ." approach, basically letting the dancers do the creating for the choreographer. In fact, this is a very common, popular method of working. The unfortunate aspect is that the dancers are rarely credited with having generated most of the movement material. This is a good person to work with if you enjoy contributing your ideas and enjoy trying out variations that are suggested by an outside eye, but you are less comfortable with making aesthetic decisions yourself. If you have respect for a choreographer's artistic vision and are proud to have played a part in contributing to that vision, this is a good choreographer for you to seek out.

## The Collaborator

Collaboration is a long, sometimes tedious, and often frustrating process. It involves listening and compromising, respecting other ideas and letting go of the notion of personal ownership of an artistic product. In true collaboration all ideas are weighed equally and, through consensus, are either trashed or incorporated into the final project. In a true collaboration there is no director, no individual who holds ultimate artistic control. This is a good process to pursue if you are a person who enjoys having your opinions and solutions reflected in the final product. This is not a good process to pursue if you are in a hurry to get something done. Nor is this a good process to pursue if you wish to receive public credit for specific contributions you have made to the final product. That's not part of this bargain.

## The Amalgamated Choreographer

You will find aspects of each of these types in most choreographers, yourself included. When learning to work with others, both as a choreographer and as a participant in other people's work, it can be helpful to recognize what styles and what power structures work best for you so that you can be clear in your dealings with others and make the most of your time together. If you really do need other people's input in order to have an original thought, it is going to speed your process by communicating that. If, on the other hand, you really need your dancers' patient and diligent effort to realize your vision, this, too, needs to be understood.

None of these styles is wrong or right. Choreography is an individual matter. To create your own dances, be aware of your own style, and choose to work with choreographers and dancers who help you grow. Perhaps you will try allying yourself with someone who insists on a specific execution of movement in order to break your movement habits. Perhaps you will choose to work with someone who gives dancers more responsibility, in order to challenge inventiveness. By paying close attention (not judgment, but attention!) to the way other students work and move, yet another valuable resource for composition will be open to you.

## "Composition Strategies I Have Known"

You have your resources, and you have your assignment. Now what?

You jump in with both feet. You draw your floor plan, you create your 4 shapes (or 40 shapes, depending on the assignment), you create your sequence of times, or you begin wherever you can imagine to begin. Often your teacher will supply you with a flowchart that breaks the creative process into bite-sized chunks. Here is an example of a process that uses an ordinary gesture, such as a handshake or a wave, as the basis of a short dance.

1. Choose a gesture.
2. Make it faster or slower than normal.
3. Make it travel.
4. Make it change level twice.
5. Create a short, patterned phrase of movement from these experiments.
6. Teach your pattern to another person.
7. Do your patterns, but maintain contact with a partner.

To help you get started, your teacher may have provided you with an order to follow—a form—to build your dance study. In the beginning, these directions can be very helpful in leading you to a finished product. But in real life, there is no recipe for creativity. Creative works come from a motivated commitment to say something. Following someone else's recipe may help you discover that you have something to say, but the product will be different if you can find a way to identify your original thoughts.

How about taking direction from your peers? If you have worked in a group, you may have discovered that as a group you had too many ideas about where to start, what to do, and how to end. Think back to some of your group work.

➡ Whose ideas were used?

➡ What process was used to make those decisions?

➡ How did you feel about having your ideas accepted, rejected, or altered?

➡ Overall, do you prefer working with a group, a partner, or on your own?

Written planning may have been useful to you. As mentioned above, it can help to draw out your floor plan both to see if you have become stuck in one place on stage and to make a map for later reference. Another strategy for organizing your thoughts may have been to write out a shorthand description of the important events of your study.

Two dancers, A and B:

1. A and B begin crouched together.
2. A rises and runs to the back (upstage).
3. B rolls to the side.
4. A falls and rolls toward B.
5. B tries to rise but only gets halfway up.
6. A clings to B, pulls B back to the floor.
7. A and B end crouched together again.

This method can also be useful for providing an overall look at what the dance is about. In addition, by playing with the language in such a description, you can often discover or create a fresh, new dance! Try filling in the blanks in a way that creates a new dance different from the first example.

Two dancers, A and B:

1. A and B begin _____ together.
2. A _____ and runs to the back (upstage).
3. B _____ to _____.
4. A falls and _____ B.
5. B tries to _____ but only _____.
6. A _____ B and _____ B _____.
7. A and B end _____.

Last, but not least, is the strategy known as the deadline. The dance project is due, you make some decisions, you trot out the same old movements, you string them together, and you do your best to perform what you remember. (This is the generic solo. Just as your supermarket carries things like detergent and cleanser with no particular brand, you can create a dance that has no particular brand.) You know it is not your best work, but . . . well . . . you just ran out of time to create something really special.

If you have ever found yourself out of time and still unprepared, the rest of this chapter is for you. If you have ever been disappointed with the dances you have presented, read on. The art and process of making a statement through dance is similar to the art and process of any synthesis of thought or materials. There is play involved, and there is discipline. There is adventure in exploring many options, and there is patience required to redefine the focus of the statement you wish to make. We have reviewed some of the resources, processes, and strategies you have probably used, consciously or subconsciously, when preparing your dance compositions. Having an original dance thought is not too different from writing an original essay or creating an original painting.

## Getting Started

the creative process

Composition in any art is rarely linear; it rarely occurs in a nice, straight line. More often you will begin, change your mind, start somewhere else, collect more information (thoughts, images, sounds), add, subtract, and so on. This process of beginning can go on as long as time and patience allow. One choreographer might brood over a piece for two or three years. Another might have only 45 minutes to stage a piece, so decisions need to be made quickly. Your creative schedule will depend on how and when you will be evaluated.

We have all had some experience with the creative process used in writing, so consider that as a model for the process of creating in dance. In writing, there are six stages of composition:

1. Prewrite
2. Make notes
3. Draft
4. Rewrite
5. Polish
6. Publish (Hand in!)

The prewrite stage is like shopping. Let us say you know you are going to need a new jacket in the next couple of months. Gradually you become very aware of jackets. You find yourself looking at the jackets strangers wear or you are mysteriously drawn to the jacket department of any clothing store you pass. The world becomes a sea of jackets. In this shopping stage, you tune yourself to news and information about your field or your subject. You make yourself receptive. You talk to people. You do not necessarily *write* anything. You simply collect. In dance, the prewrite stage is the time for using all your senses to take in any and all information about your field of interest. Study other people, look at animals and insects, look for accidental patterns, lines, coincidences. Close your eyes and sense. Experiment and improvise without a plan; just do it for fun.

Next comes the time for taking notes. This is the stage where your personality starts to play a part in the creative process. What do *you* find interesting? What connections do *you* make with your life and your subject? Someone says something interesting, and you write it down or ask for a reference. You go to the library and read through books, magazines, or whatever resources will give you that spark, central theme, or focus. This is the stage where you allow the material to grab *you*. In dance, the note-taking stage is the time for writing, for collecting pictures, for gathering music, clothing, and related things that have to do with your field.

When your notebook is full, your pockets are stuffed with scraps of ideas, and your desk or work space is cluttered with related materials, you will feel close to having something to say for all your research. You begin to draft. In dance, this is the stage where you begin to set movement patterns that are close to feeling right.

In writing, some people begin by making an outline. Some people might begin by modeling their writing after the pattern of another author. (But remember, the writing process began long before!) This is often the most difficult stage of the creative process because, in spite of all the resources that have been gathered, people *still* lack the confidence to recognize what it is that they find interesting about a subject.

In dance the problem is often the same. Young choreographers come to the studio forgetting that the process of choreography began on the street, in their daydreams, the checkout line, the library, and in their classes; they need those resources to begin their first choreographic draft. In any creative process, it is a mistake to attempt to leap straight from the assignment to the final product. That would be like expecting to pour a jigsaw puzzle out of the box directly into its completed form. What fun would *that* be?

After you create your written rough draft, you breathe a sigh of relief, and you set your work aside so that you can return to it with fresh eyes a little later. Your rewrite stage may include getting feedback from friends or family. Or perhaps you feel confident in your abilities to rework your composition on your own—cutting out the fat or adding necessary examples. Add another check to make sure all your spelling is right, punctuation is in order, and the overall appearance is kind to the reader, and it is ready to hand in!

In dance you might ask a friend to watch and give you feedback, or you might even teach your work to another dancer to see if he can make it say what you want your work to say. If you are lucky enough to have access to a video camera, you can tape your work and do your own editing. In dance, feedback and review are *critical* to the creative process. As a performing art, dance is meant to be shared. Critical feedback is, therefore, a vital part of the choreographic process. Unlike shopping for and eventually buying a jacket, in dance, you are never stuck with something that no longer fits or no longer feels fashionable. The creative process is ongoing and is fed by your new ideas and the reactions and ideas of your audiences.

Let us look for similarities in the creative process used in painting. First the painter collects and stores images, shapes, colors, contrasts, textures, and relationships. She talks about what she plans to do and receives feedback. She makes notes and sketches; she looks back at her earlier work and at the ways other artists have treated the same subject that she is considering. She must also prepare her canvas. How big will the surface be? What shape will the surface be? What kind of surface will be appropriate? Then she begins. She paints, she erases, she over-paints, she leaves it in the corner for a while, she looks at it every day, she talks to it, she allows a few, close friends a peek, she works on it some more, and, eventually, she feels that she has captured all the piece was meant to contain. She has made her statement. A few more touches, and it is ready to be framed!

## Six Stages of the Creative Process

When we described the creative process for writing and painting we assumed that a subject or field of interest had already been identified. The sentences referred to collecting images almost as if these images could be found scattered about like leaves or stones. In a sense, they are. Your motivation for a dance can come from many sources: an assignment, a piece of music, a dream, a feeling, an event witnessed or experienced. In fact, any aspect of life that has motivated you is fair game for treatment in dance. Later we will discuss the ways in which some subjects may be more suitable than others, but for now, let us keep focusing just on process and make a direct comparison of the writing process to the process of dance composition.

| *Writing* | *Dance* |
|-----------|---------|
| 1. Prewrite | 1. Collect |
| 2. Make notes | 2. Note and improvise |
| 3. Draft | 3. Choose and develop movement material |
| 4. Rewrite | 4. Rework material |
| 5. Polish | 5. Rehearse and refine |
| 6. Publish | 6. Perform |

### Collecting

Think back to chapter 9 on perception. Take a general concept, and try to experience this concept in every sense. In the movie *Tap*, the main character explains to a crowd the process his famous father used to invent new tap steps: "He took the sounds from the street," he says, and has the crowd listen to the rhythms of the passing cars, the pumps, the whistles, and, in short, the city life. You may not pick up the beat quite as quickly as the cast of the movie, but the point remains valid. You can begin by using your senses and all three perceptual modes to collect all kinds of great material that is *yours*—unique to you and original.

### Noting and Improvising

Begin to make notes, draw pictures, collect samples, record dreams, and generally catalogue the relevant images you discover.

As your collection of notes, pictures, samples, dreams, and other relevant images builds, allow yourself a time and a place to improvise with these images.

**Begin to clarify the gift you hope to make with your work.**

This can be a difficult step. The challenge here is to define the problem, not the solution. Perhaps the problem has already been defined for you. For instance, your assignment is to make a dance using curved and straight pathways. That is a perfectly valid problem, but probably not one you can get too excited about, unless you create *your own* problem to make things interesting (both for you and your audience). Here are some examples of how you might use your sense inventory to explore the assignment:

1. <u>Sight</u>—Trace the outline of a tree's branches in winter, and let that be your floor plan.

2. <u>Sound</u>—In an urban setting, time the intervals between the honking of horns or the passing of cars; let the length of those intervals determine how long you will move in a straight path and when you will change to a contrasting curve. In a rural setting, you might use the rhythm of wood being chopped or the bark of a dog.

3. <u>Taste</u>—Soft foods mush (How could a pathway be made to dissolve?). Chewy foods require indirect effort (Maybe a zigzag pattern?). A mouthful of peas pop and explode as they are chewed. A pizza has to be dragged and pulled apart.

4. <u>Touch</u>—Collect five objects. Put them in a sack. If you are right-handed, then hold a pen in your left hand. (Vice versa for lefties.) Close your eyes. With the hand you usually use for writing, pick one of the objects from the sack. Using your other hand draw a line of texture based on whatever you have pulled from the bag. Make one continuous line—your straight and curving-path dance.

5. <u>Smell</u>—What path would you take to someone wearing a lovely perfume? What path would you take to discover who had stepped in something a bit stinky? What path would you take to determine the source of a burning smell? (Remember, this is a study about pathways, not a study about leading with your nose!)

6. <u>Kinesthetic</u>—What is it like to move through a crowd to reach a friend? What kind of pathway do you follow on a walk in the woods? What path would you take to the cafeteria?

7. <u>Vestibular</u>—Close your eyes, spin around about 10 times, and try to walk in a straight line (keeping your eyes closed). Close your eyes and try to go from your bedroom to your front door, being aware of your path and how you are moving on it. No hands! Devise a movement phrase, such as swing-swing-suspend-drop. Do this phrase with your eyes closed, and allow yourself to move through space. Record the pathways generated by your different momentums.

8. <u>Organic</u>—Does hunger have a pathway? Nausea? Warmth? Relaxation? Cramps? Stretches? Sure they do!

At this stage of the creative process, you do not need to know exactly what you are going to say. You need only to be open to many different aspects of your subject, to discover what it is you have to offer and what makes you enthusiastic. You are not shopping for an answer; you are shopping for a problem.

**You are looking for an aspect of the world you wonder about.**

The problem you identify—the focus you select—will be your working focus. This may or may not be your final focus, but it will provide you with a place to start refining your thoughts and drafting what it is you would like to say. When you have defined at least two interesting problems, you are ready to move on to drafting one or more solutions.

## Choosing and Developing Your Focus

Now we get to the question of form and intent. What, exactly, do you want your dance to *do* to the audience? Let us say (and hope) that you have done your research, you have established that there is something in the world that you would like to comment on, and now you must decide: What is the function I would like this piece to serve? What is the focus of this piece? The answers to these questions will lead you to the most appropriate structure of your material.

➡ Is there a *specific message* you would like to deliver?

Drugs are bad for you.

A dog is my best friend.

A bear can kill you.

➡ Is there a *feeling* you would like to deliver?

When I am in love, I feel like I can fly.

I wish I could help.

I will never be picked for anything.

➡ Is there an *opinion* or a *realization* you want to share?

People are like animals in the way they treat each other.

A person can have many friends but still be alone.

Events outside our control shape our lives.

Your choice of structure will depend on the function you would like your piece to serve. The same is true in written and in painted communication.

Suppose you have an assignment to write a paper on an article that you have been asked to read. If the function of your paper is to show the teacher that you read the article, then you rephrase the opening paragraph, pull out a few quotes from the middle, and rephrase the closing paragraphs. You take the information in the article, report it in your own words, and hand it in without adding new information. This level of response does indicate to the teacher that you have read the article. It does not give the teacher any idea about how you felt about the subject, what else you might know about the subject, or what kinds of experiences you can add to the author's point of view. To go to this second level requires a little more thought and investment on your part. At this deeper level, you would identify relationships that you had discovered in your reading. Perhaps you have found another article on the same subject, and you can make comparisons. Perhaps you have direct experience with the subject, and you

## Figure 10.1
Rembrandt van Rijn's "Aristotle With a Bust of Homer."

include your own observations. The first kind of report is an example of a response on a literal level. The second, in-depth response would be called an interpretive response. There is one more level to go: the evaluative. In a paper written on this level, you would quickly establish the author's point of view and then spend most of your time explaining the effect the article had on you. Suppose it is an article about Vietnam veterans returning to their homes. You might be moved to write a poem or a story of your own. You might find a veteran to interview. You might make a collage of images and slogans from that time. In short, you use the information in the assigned article as a jumping-off point for creating your own opinion. You have an original thought, and you make an original statement based on your experience.

These three levels are sometimes described in this way:

*Literal*—Restating what is there

*Interpretive*—Restating what is there *and* pointing out relationships you observe

*Evaluative*—Restating what is there *and* creating new relationships not already suggested

In painting you will also find three ways of interpreting a subject. A painter may copy an image as closely as possible (Figure 10.1), may change some aspect of the subject for a particular effect (Figure 10.2), or may create a completely new form to go with a unique point of view about the subject (Figure 10.3).

## Figure 10.2
Pablo Picasso's "Nude With Pitcher."

**Figure 10.3**
Jackson Pollack's "Autumn Rhythm."

None of these three approaches is any better—or even any more sophisticated—than another. The choice of structure depends on what the artist wants to accomplish. The form will follow the function. If a painter wants us to appreciate the beauty of a particular landscape, then a painting that is as accurate as possible will best serve the purpose. If a painter wants to communicate passion or desperation, then the source material may not even be represented! We may only see colors, lines, and unidentified forms.

Now back to dance. What names would you use to describe these three approaches to forming a dance statement? Look at the list of words below, and choose the three words that best describe the three solutions one might use to solve a dance problem:

| Imitate | Copy | Report | Duplicate |
| Express | Infer | Interpret | Figure |
| Invent | Evaluate | Abstract | Imply |

Keeping these three levels of solutions in our minds, let us return to the creative process and apply them. Suppose your class is studying qualities and how to use different movement qualities to achieve a desired choreographic effect.

> **Your assignment: Create a solo based on two contrasting movement qualities.**

Where do you begin? With the first stage of creating: collecting. You open yourself up to the world of qualities. You tune in to the qualities of everyday things around you. Trees, rocks, dogs, buzzers, songs, fabrics, candies, crowds, and buildings are all source material for a study on qualities. Rough, heavy, furry, piercing, tender, soft, energizing, jarring, and majestic are all qualities (and there will be thousands more!) that come directly from your life.

Your next step is to make notes. Movements, feelings, thrills, fears, comfort, pain, and sensations are all saved for future reference and development. On to narrowing your focus. Identify the most important or most interesting aspects of your exploration of quality.

Let us say you choose the contrast between tight and loose. Who knows why? It might be that the contrast kept jumping out at you during your collection process. Go back through your notes, back through your sense and perception inventories, to rediscover all that you already know about these qualities in your life.

Then apply the three levels of abstraction we discussed above to determine what you want your study to accomplish. Until you have experimented with all three structures, it will be hard to decide which is most appropriate. Here are some examples of how you might define a tight-loose dance problem within each of the structures:

1. Imitate

   ➡ I want to present the different tension patterns I have observed in people at school—how they hold themselves, how they walk, how they stand, and so on. I will imitate these people and collect them into one dance.

   ➡ I want to present the importance of balancing tension in the body while practicing technique. I will imitate a dance student who is completely tense and will make my point by letting one body part become loose, then tense again when another body part becomes loose. In the end, I will be a loose heap on the floor.

   ➡ I want to present the range of going from completely loose to completely tight. I will imitate water gradually freezing solid.

2. Interpret

   ➡ I want the audience to sense the limitations of tension and relaxation. My dance will be a straight line across the floor, and each step will either be completely tight or completely loose; progress will be difficult.

3. Invent

   ➡ I want the audience to see that tight does not necessarily mean strong, and loose does not necessarily mean floppy or weak. I will design movements to show that tight, taken to its extreme, becomes weak, and looseness, taken to its extreme, becomes very strong.

   ➡ I want the audience to draw its own conclusions about these two extremes. I will present a series of duets where one dancer is very loose and the partner is very tight. Then I will reverse their roles and repeat the entire dance.

## Refining and Redefining Your Focus

The final stage of getting started occurs when you can look at all your exploratory material and say, "This is it!"

"This is the subject I feel most compelled to present."

"This will be a gift from me to the world."

"This is my original thought."

In the reworking stage, be prepared to do some major house-cleaning. That is, look at the material you have created and decide if that material you have created hangs together as a whole and if aspects need to be modified or eliminated. This stage is a bit like spring cleaning—a good time to throw out things you do not really use, put a shine on things you truly love, and store things that no longer belong where they have been.

Sometimes the reworking stage loops you right back to the beginning of the creative process. Sometimes the reworking stage requires little more than a few small modifications.

## Rehearsing

Rehearsal. It seems a person either loves it or hates it. If what you love about the choreographic process is the magic of the discovery of a dance, then repeating and refining the actual steps and sequences can seem mundane. If you are the sort who endures the creative process in order to be able to enjoy working with the completed sequences, then rehearsal is the icing on the cake for you.

In the immortal words of John Cage, musician and philosopher, "If you find something boring, do it again." The rehearsal stage can be an exciting and immensely satisfying stage of the creative process, and, yes, it can be very creative. This is the time when the soul of the performer can expand into the material that has been formed.

Getting started can last as long as time and patience allow. As you become more skilled at collecting and as you develop your powers of perception, you will probably discover that dance subjects and dance problems come to you often. Having an idea will no longer be a problem, but selecting among many dance-worthy ideas may prove challenging!

In the next chapter we will discuss forming your dance problem into a well-developed piece. When making your choice among your possible focuses, consider a few, final questions:

Is your problem a dance problem? In *The Art of Making Dances*, Doris Humphrey, a pioneer of modern dance, opened her chapter on theme with these words:

> No matter what the subject, the first test to apply is one word—action. Does the theme have inherently the motivation for movement? At all times we must be aware that the dance art is unique in its medium of movement (along with mime, a sister art). Unique, too, is its power to evoke emotion within its vocabulary, to arouse the kinetic sense, to speak of the subtleties of the body and soul. But the language has definite limitations and should not be forced to communicate beyond its range, which is, again, that part of experience which can be expressed in physical action. (p. 34)

You can also apply the test of description. Can you describe, using words, the substance of your piece? Do you find that your description fails to capture the essence of your focus? In short, if a song, poem, painting, or essay can be used to *fully* capture the essence of your thought, then write a song, poem, essay, or paint the picture. If you are using any of these sources as a springboard for your ideas (as is often the case with music), *be sure* that your work adds to the art which already exists. Acting out the words to a song might be useful if the song is being played for people who speak a different language or for people who are deaf, but, in most cases, it is not necessary to act out lyrics.

There are three important questions to ask yourself before developing your thought into a piece:

1. Have you identified a dance problem?
2. Can the problem be best solved in the medium of dance?
3. Are you bringing new information to light?

If all your answers are positive, move on to the dance!

## Think About It

1. What, for you, is the most frustrating part about making dances? What is the most pleasurable part of making dances?

2. What would you say is the part of your dance class that you do best? Are you good at balancing? Good at turning? Do you feel your arms move smoothly? Do you do well in movement across the floor? How do you see that, or those, strengths reflected in your composition work?

   a. Now consider the part of class that you dread.

   b. Think about parallels these preferences have in other parts of your life. In general, do you prefer a fast or a slow pace? Do you prefer situations where you are pretty much in control, or do you prefer situations where there might be surprises?

   c. Think about the type of choreographer that you are most inclined to work with.

3. The next time you attend a social function where there is social dancing, stand back and observe the kinds of movement most people are making when they dance. Where did these movements come from? Consider the fact that two years ago people moved in a different way. Imagine how people would have danced in this kind of occasion 50 years ago, or 100 years ago. Why do these dances change, and how do people know to change their dancing? What role does media play in popularizing a way of dancing? Could you (yes, *you!*) invent a new social dance?

# 11

# Composition

**C**omposition is the process of creating form by bringing related pieces together. Purpose guides the process of composition. For instance, a mechanic could take all the pieces of an engine and assemble them so that they have an interesting look or assemble them so that they create a functioning engine. Both compositions are valid; they just have different purposes. We would call one a sculpture and the other an engine, and we would have different expectations for each composition (Figure 11.1).

Like a mechanic or a sculptor, a choreographer brings together related movements to compose dances. The form that this composition takes will depend on the purpose the choreographer intends to fulfill with the dance. Whether these mechanical, sculptural, or choreographic forms are successful in conveying the ideas that the composers had in mind will depend on their understanding of the three primary considerations of composition: function, materials, and audience.

## Function

The mechanic trying to rebuild an engine that will power a car safely and quietly has to know how an engine works, what order in which to assemble the pieces, what pieces can be used again, and which need to be replaced. A good mechanic also is sensitive to the interests of the car owner (the audience) and needs to find out whether the owner wants to spend the money necessary to create a new engine or to get by as cheaply as possible.

## Figure 11.1

An unconventional but technically functional teapot by contemporary artist Kathy Triplett.

The sculptor using the engine parts to create art does not need to know about how an engine works. The sculptor does need to decide what the purpose of this collection of engine parts should be. A funny-looking engine-shaped sculpture? A frightening engine-like sculpture? A sculpture that bears no resemblance to an engine at all? Once those decisions have been made, the sculptor works with the available pieces in any order, using the pieces that the sculptor likes and leaving out others. A piece that might normally belong inside a working engine might work better *for an aesthetic purpose* on the outside.

The sculptor's composition may also be guided by the intended audience. Will this be seen from all sides? Will people be able to climb or sit on this? Should this fit in someone's living room? Should this fit on someone's coffee table? If the mechanic regularly ignores the interests of the audience—the customers—that mechanic will probably go out of business. On the other hand, the sculptor could choose to be the only audience for the work and simply create for the pleasure of composition.

The choreographer uses life experiences to create dances in much the same way that both the sculptor and the mechanic compose their products. By developing training and skills using the tools of the trade, and by applying the principles of form and function (what it is supposed to look like and what it is supposed to do), the choreographer becomes engaged in the process of composition.

A dance can be created to serve several functions: to tell a story, to showcase a particular skill, to express an insight, to entertain, to arouse, to explore, and an infinite list of others—all are valid functions for a dance.

## Materials

The materials of dance must come from the choreographer's experience. Perceptions, sensations, feelings, and ideas all add up to having a perspective that one wishes to share with the world. Along with having something to say, a choreographer will benefit from developing physical skills that allow the widest possible range of movement choices. In addition, it helps to have a basic understanding of some of the theories of composition. Just as the mechanic needs to understand the theories associated with the workings of an internal-combustion engine, and how the parts are supposed to fit together, likewise, a choreographer needs to understand some basic composition theories.

## Audience

Finally, the choreographer needs to consider the audience that will, hopefully, be touched by the dance. Like both the mechanic and the sculptor, the choreographer needs to be clear about the interests of the audiences likely to view the dance. The choreographer also needs to decide how important it is that an audience precisely understands the work. If the mechanic's audience (the customers) does not understand what they have paid for, they are likely not to come back with their business. If the sculptor's work fails to attract audiences that understand the work, that sculptor will not be recognized by enough people to become famous. Even though the sculptor may still enjoy the creative process, that sculptor must accept recognition from only a small audience.

If a choreographer's audiences do not understand what the dance is trying to say, they are likely not to seek out the work again. The choreographer may enjoy making dances anyway and be pleased by pleasing a more select audience (Figure 11.2). If an audience has likely never seen any dance before, its members are likely to react to a very

**Figure 11.2**
The choreographer may be pleased by pleasing a more select audience.

sensual dance the only way they know how to react, that is, to draw from their experiences of other public performances of sensuality. An attempt at humor may fall flat on an audience that has not seen enough dance to understand why something is humorous. Similarly, an audience, regardless of its sophistication, will be quickly bored by choreography that lacks content, direction, or craft. Stepping back and asking yourself, "What is it that I want the audience to see?" can be a helpful way to direct your work and to evaluate its success.

As we explore the process of composition we will look at principles that apply to creating not only good dances but also effective speeches, insightful lab reports, and compelling writing assignments. Without going too far out on a limb, you could even make a case for applying the principles of composition to some of your personal relationships. What we are aiming at here is the development of your abilities to be able to communicate your perceptions, sensations, feelings, and ideas as effectively as possible. Whether this means you build engines, sculptures, or dances does not matter. To this process, the process of composition, there is an art.

## Arranger or Composer?

In the flower-delivery business there are books that you as a customer can look at to choose the arrangement you wish to send to a loved one across the country. You can go into a shop in Cleveland, Ohio, point to a picture, pay the bill, and know that exactly that arrangement can and will be created by a florist in Topeka, Kansas. The designs you choose from are designs that have proven to be very popular over the years, so the floral industry has standardized them. Is the florist who gets the order in Topeka an arranger or a composer?

A man is cleaning out his basement and decides, in order to make his job more fun, he will nail, glue, tie, or somehow attach together the things that he decides are now junk and make a table. Old boards, pieces of plastic, empty jugs, odd lengths of rope, dried-up paint cans, broken tools, and a dead lawn mower are attached as they are discovered. The product is about 6 feet wide, 4 feet tall, and really has very few level surfaces on which anything could be placed. Nevertheless, he set out to make a table, so that is what he calls his final product. Is this table maker an arranger or a composer?

A dance student has paid close attention in technique class and has learned to execute many exciting movements and sequences presented by the teacher. She is a good dancer because she picks up steps quickly and imitates them very accurately. Making up dances comes fairly easily to her because she has mastered so many exciting sequences; she simply strings several of these together and voilà! A dance! Is this dancer an arranger or a composer?

Arranger or composer? How are these roles different? This question particularly plagues beginning composition students because they are the ones who tend to feel most insecure about their abilities to create anything original. As we discussed in the previous chapter, original thought is something that emerges when you trust your own experience and bring some aspect of yourself to your creative efforts. Have you ever found yourself in a creative void, rejecting a movement or sequence because it has been

Winton Marsalis, a famous musician, once kidded a young student about being "hip," saying that to be hip was to have a limited number of responses to a maximum number of circumstances. He was pointing out that, if a musician is going to make music that comes from the soul, the musician has to dig into the soul to find that music.

done a million times? Have you ever been frustrated because you feel you are nothing but an arranger and you want to be a composer?

It is the aim of this chapter to get you over that chasm, to provide you with the tools to shape your work and be able to use the materials of dance to compose in a personally satisfying way. These materials are not new; they have been reworked for centuries. It is not your job to discover the elements of dance, nor is it necessary to reinvent the art form. A composer, sculptor, musician, or mechanic is simply responsible for integrating life experiences through composition.

## The Discovery of Form

Someone offers you a hand in greeting, and you respond by extending your own. But when, in an emergency, someone extends his hand to you in desperation you first respond by bracing your entire body and *then* extend your own hand. The form of your response to the world is based on your life experience. Think back to the primary considerations of composition we discussed at the beginning of this chapter—function, materials, audience—and to how those three considerations are automatically part of your ability to respond to both of these situations.

From the Latin *integer*, meaning "whole" or "entire," comes the verb "integrate," to form into a whole, to unite with something else. You are uniquely capable of that formation based on your unique way of being response-able. As a choreographer you feel, perceive, sense, and, from those responses, discover an integration of those responses that is your own form.

Have you ever had an experience you looked back on and thought, "I can't believe I *did* that!" Well, whatever it was that you did was an act of forming, of responding to and integrating your life experience. Your discovery of that form may have filled you with pride, embarrassment, or excitement, but regardless of how you later evaluated your experience, the point here is that you *discovered* a form of response which most likely came to you in that particular moment.

That is what the discovery of form in choreography is about. The discovery happens in the doing, in the moment, when you are trying one thing and something else happens that relates to something else, that reminds you of something else, or that turns into something else.

We began this chapter by identifying three primary considerations in composing—function, materials, and audience. We then pointed out that there is a difference between arranging and composing. Composing requires an active response to your world using what you know and what you suspect. From this active, response-able, integrating position, you will discover a form that makes sense—visual, auditory, and kinesthetic sense. This discovery of form is the beginning of the creative process. From this beginning the choreographer continues by exploring other aspects of the form. What emerges in that process of exploration are the important ideas or, in the case of dance, the movements that will define the dance.

## Theme

A theme is a composition structure, a unifying idea. Parties have themes—The Roaring 20s, The 1950s. Conventions have themes—The Asphalt Pavers Annual Meeting, The National Organization of Women Convention. Courses have themes—Contemporary African Politics, Western Attitudes Toward Death and Dying. You know what a theme is, but you may not have considered it in terms of choreography. When we refer to a *theme* in choreography, we mean something more specific than the basic idea, mood, or general heading. In choreography,

> **A theme is a sequence of movements that are recognizable as a sequence.**

In choreography, a theme is not announced as it is with parties, conventions, and courses. The title may hint at the mood (solitude), the period (ragtime), or the content of the dance (*Swan Lake*), but it does not reveal a theme. The theme is established as the dance unfolds. It is established through repetition and contrast. When the same sequence occurs over and over, the audience is able to recognize the movement and look at subtle differences in the presentation of the movement; they understand what idea is being developed through the dance.

Building on a theme is a bit like displaying a crystal. You choose what facets of the crystal are most interesting to look at or what will produce the most interesting patterns in the light. When you hold a crystal up to the light, you make rainbows, dots, sparkles, or streamers. You choose the kind of patterns you want to make by the way you choose to display the crystal.

a unifying idea

A dance can be composed of a single repeating sequence that recurs throughout the dance, or it can be composed of several related sequences that show different facets of the same concept. As an example, let us make up a short movement theme:

**step     close     step     hop-turn     shake**

Five actions. One way you might establish this as a theme is to begin your dance by having each of five dancers enter solo by identically performing this sequence. Or you could have each one enter solo doing the sequence but varying the timing. Or you could have them enter as a group and split off as solos. Or you could . . . . What else could you do to begin a dance by introducing this theme?

What do you remember from earlier chapters that you could apply to this process of thematic development? How about varying aspects of the time, space, or effort involved with the theme? How about using a pattern found in nature, the rhythm of a poem, or the code of your phone number?

As long as the elements of the sequence remain in the same order, as long as that order remains intact, you are still working with the same theme. Note also that this theme is defined strictly by a series of movements, not by a mood, a costume, or a particular sentiment. All those aspects of a dance are certainly valid, but they are outside the realm of the theme as it is being defined here.

## Motif

To return to the dance we have been building, let us suppose the first five dancers make their solo entrances identically repeating the phrase, and a sixth dancer enters by stepping on stage and tossing the head to the side. The other dancers pick up this head toss and use it to signal each other, to indicate disapproval, and to indicate condemnation. The dance ends with one of the dancers being rejected and killed by the others. Not the loveliest scenario, but certainly a valid dance outline. Throughout, the dancers might or might not stick strictly to the movement theme we defined. The important element for the audience to keep track of is the head toss and how it evolves. The head toss is a *motif*.

A motif is the movement (or movements) that an audience will remember as characteristic to your piece: arms together and shoulders up, poking hands, swooping stage crosses, and so on.

**A theme is varied. A motif is developed.**

Think of someone you know who has a distinctive personal mannerism. Like maybe this person like overuses the word like. Or maybe this person frequently says "y'know." Think of someone you know who you could characterize with a single phrase or gesture. That is a motif.

Now think of someone you know who has a habit that you could adopt to characterize this person. Maybe this person is usually late and wastes a lot of time making excuses. Maybe this person is sensitive to dirt and regularly washes, fusses, and cleans up before sitting down. If there is a pattern of behavior that would characterize this person, that pattern would better be referred to as a theme than a motif.

The only reason to think about the difference between a theme and a motif is that it can be helpful to know what you expect the audience to pick up so that they understand your work. The more you can identify what is important, the easier it will be for an audience to understand.

## Principles of Composition

There are seven principles of composition that guide the creation of a dance. But remember, these same principles are going to apply to creating other kinds of compositions too. Different critics and art reviewers may compose their lists differently, but the following seven principles will serve as a useful reference:

1. Contrast
2. Repetition
3. Transition
4. Variation
5. Development
6. Climax
7. Resolution

### Contrast

> "A juxtaposition of . . . color, tone, or emotion in a work of art."
> —Merriam Webster's Collegiate Dictionary, Tenth edition

*Contrast* is a diversity of color, emotion, or tone. It is the green of the leaves that makes the yellow of the daffodil especially bright. Contrast intensifies experiences.

In order to keep your dance from becoming monotonous, the audience needs a break—in speed of the movement, intensity, level, direction (or draw), and quality. Have you ever had a teacher who spoke in a monotone? If so, you may remember the difficulty you had staying awake in that class. The same thing goes for dances. Without the principle of contrast, you are going to put your audience to sleep.

Sharp movements are sharper when juxtaposed with soft or sustained movements. Small gestures become more intimate when contrasted with large movements. Leaps seem even higher when they begin or end at a low level. Explore this principle of contrast for yourself by trying an experiment.

Think of a color and a simple, repeating movement that you can do in association with that color. Find two other movements that occur on different levels and are also associated with that color. Perform them in a series. (If you are sitting in a library and do not want to risk being thrown out for dancing in the stacks, you can still experiment with this by using just your hands!) Call that series A.

*contrast intensifies experiences*

To make series B, go through the same process but with a different color that most radically contrasts with your first choice. Find a simple, repeating movement, then add two other related movements to this B sequence. Perform your contrasting statements as ABA. How does the feel of your composition change if you rearrange the sequence as A1 B1 A2 B2 A3 B3? Which do you prefer? Think about function and audience. As simple as these compositions are, what might be the function of each (what does each say)? Could you vary that function by varying the time, space, or effort involved? What would the members of an audience need to see to make that contrast as effective as possible? Would they need to be very close? Would they need to be able to see your face? How would this work change if it were performed on a football field? If performed by 30 people at the same time? Contrasts can evolve. They can involve shading a movement or a phrase just enough so that there is a perceptible difference from the previous effort or intention. Black and white contrasts can be effective, and so can black, gray, and white. There is neither a formula nor a limit to one's method of creating contrast.

> Contrast can be a good starting place if you are stuck for a way to begin a composition assignment. Pick any set of opposites to use as a basis for improvisation, and you will probably discover some interesting material. Here is a preliminary list:
>
> | | | |
> |---|---|---|
> | open-close | high-low | fast-slow |
> | here-there | fight-flight | in-out |
> | hard-soft | hot-cold | horizontal-vertical |

Let us go back to your experiment above and rework your A phrase so that all three parts evolve rather than slam into your B phrase. Instead of making all three A moves as hard as possible and all three B moves as soft as possible, find a way to go from hard to soft more gradually so that the contrast is still there but it is more subtle. Reevaluate your work. Does one method of contrast make more sense than the other? Does another method now occur to you?

## Repetition

> **"You got to give your audience something to hang onto."**
> **—John Coltrane**

Your movement idea can be developed, varied, reversed, slowed down, speeded up, stood on its head, and just about completely distorted, but as long as the members of the audience have some clue about what you, the choreographer, have identified as important, they will be able to sense what your work is about. One way to emphasize the things that are important is to repeat them. By repeating a sequence, a phrase, a floor pattern, or even one simple gesture you give the audience clues as to what is tying your dance together. Let us look at how *repetition* is used to assist audiences of other presentations.

Repetition is another good starting place if you are stuck for a way to get going on a composition. It is also a good device to use when feeling pressured to be inventive. By limiting your options for invention, you are likely to discover some of the nuances of a phrase, theme, or motif that might have escaped you if you had moved on to new material. Here are a few structures for repetition that you may find useful:

- Repeat in a different body part.
- Repeat in a different facing.
- Repeat at a different speed.
- Repeat at a different level.
- Repeat with different force.
- Repeat either accelerating or decelerating.

The standard three-part recipe for speech writing is (1) tell them what you are going to say, (2) say what you are going to say, and (3) tell them what you just said. Listen for this formula next time you attend a speech or a lecture.

In pop music the chorus provides the repetition that pulls the song together. If it is a message song, the message is usually written into the part that gets repeated. If it is a love song, the lyrics that are repeated in the chorus are usually the from-the-heart part of the song. In symphonic music, a theme is created around which the whole symphony is built. To keep the different parts related, the composer will often repeat sections of the theme throughout the full-length work.

Look for repetition in architecture. Repetition of a shape or design from the outside may be repeated inside as a way of tying the look of the building together. Repetition can be used to create a sense of stability and harmony.

In dance the choreographer must strike a delicate balance between providing enough repetition so that it is clear what is going on and providing enough contrast so that the audience does not become bored. As long as you do not beat a repetition to death, it can actually be a comfort to the audience to see something familiar.

How much repetition is enough? How much is too much? Maybe you know people who tell you that they love you. If they say it too often, the phrase starts to lose its power and starts to sound like "Have a nice day." But if they hardly *ever* say "I love you" and cannot seem to say it when it is most important to you, then you might start to wonder if they really *do* love you. "And if they do," you might wonder, "why is it so hard to tell me?" As you improve in the craft of relating your ideas to other people, you will develop your own sense of how much repetition is appropriate for your statements. This sense is applicable to dance, to other artistic pursuits, and to living.

## Transition

"You can't get there from here."
—Old Minnesota saying

Another saying often heard in dance and composition classes is that the real dance occurs, not in the events (the dazzling leaps or the human tricks), but rather *between* the events of choreography. It is easy to create a string of events or activities and move from one to the other as if you became invisible between these photo opportunities. In fact, the choreography will only hang together if the performance is sustained throughout—if the movements between the movements are both important and inevitable. Just as our language is composed of nouns, verbs, adjectives, adverbs, and articles, so are dances composed by different parts of dance that contribute to the sense of the movement. We might get the basic drift of thought from a collection of words such as

### Wind Blows Tree Roots Falls Ground,

but a more complete thought includes a few transitional words:

### When Wind Blows Tree Without Roots Falls Ground.

A graceful sentence includes even more transitional words as well as some punctuation that tells the reader when and how to pause:

### When a wind blows, a tree without roots falls to the ground.

Try this experiment to get a sense of the role *transition* plays in choreography. From whatever position you are in right now as you read, prepare yourself *without moving* to stand up. Do not actually change positions yet, just prepare yourself to make this change. When you are ready, go from your reading position to a standing position in one move, simply and directly, no bracing, hauling, or pausing allowed. When you have arrived at your standing position, prepare to go directly to your former reading position again—in one move. Try these exercises without transitions now.

Modify your reading position so that it is a contained shape. You might want to wrap your arms and draw up your knees. Whatever shape you create, get ready to move to that shape from a more relaxed position. Go.

Now get on your feet and invent a movement that goes in the air, such as a jump, turn, or hop into a designed standing shape. Now, go back to your relaxed reading position and repeat these activities in this order:

1. Relaxed reading pose
2. Contained shape
3. Movement in the air
4. Relaxed reading pose

Finally, see if you can feel a difference in the performance, and in the statement made, by finding a way to connect all four events. If not, repeat the sequence and take more time between events—so that they are absolutely unrelated to each other—and work one last time through your sequence without stopping. You will start to feel what this transition business is all about!

By applying what you know about contrast and repetition, you could even build on these four activities and shapes further and make a more elaborate statement, could you not?

In the experiment you just completed, you were asked to focus on the idea of making transitions from one shape or activity to another while moving almost continuously, so that one thing flowed into or was driven by another. Let us not overlook the fact that stillness can also be a useful tool for transition. Stillness is its own kind of action. There is a difference between active stillness and careless stillness, and as a choreographer you would need to be sure that the movement you create has a history—that it comes from some source inside or outside the dancer.

Moving from stillness can be a very useful tool for getting over choreographic blocks. As we said in chapter 1, the living body is never completely still. There is always movement within, and that inner movement can be a terrific source of inspiration if one is willing to be still long enough to be inspired.

Save this next experiment for a time and place where you will have some undisturbed privacy. Your teacher may choose to talk you through this sequence in class. If not, you might want to take turns with a friend so that each of you can be guided through this experiment without having to stop and read each step for yourself. This experiment works best starting in a standing position, or at least a position from which you can move easily. If you start in a prone position, it tends to be more difficult to maintain the active stillness and easier to just take a nap.

Stand in a relaxed position, arms by your sides, knees easy, belly soft, and eyes relaxed and closed. Tune in to the circulation of blood through your body, the pull of gravity on your body, and the ever-so-slight compensations of balance you need to make on this spinning earth.

From this active stillness pay attention to your breathing. Try not to interfere with the pattern of your breathing; simply observe it as a pattern. As you inhale, your chest and belly expand, and, as you exhale, they collapse. Allow yourself to rest and be still between breaths.

Try expanding and softening the back on your next inhalation and exhalation. Repeat this expansion as long as it interests you. Try expanding and softening your left side on your next inhalation and exhalation. Repeat this expansion as long as it interests you. Explore expanding and softening different body parts of your choosing as you inhale and exhale. Repeat these expansions as long as they interest you, and remember to honor the stillness between breaths.

Without inventing, allow some part of this process of inhaling and exhaling to become more exaggerated. This is the tricky part. The tendency is to want to make something happen or do something interesting. Resist this urge to place an activity on an already active body, and allow the movement to emerge from the inside. Eventually, you may find yourself moving very vigorously. Keep relating to your breath as you literally re-inspire your movement. You may find that you are actively still for long periods. Again, keep relating to your breath pattern as you explore the subtleties of minimal movement.

You will learn from this experiment that movement is always occurring, whether or not it is outwardly visible, and that your body, if you pay attention, will guide you transitionally from what you may have thought was merely one movement to the next.

According to Martha Graham, "All action is born of necessity." Whether you choose to choreograph transitions that show a violent cause and effect, a seamless flow,

*movement is always occurring*

or no apparent relationship at all, the way you deal with transition as a principle of composition will affect your work.

## Variation

> "The most deeply instinctual aesthetic form is the A B A: the beginning, middle, and end. It is the universal pattern of life itself: we are born, we live, we return to the unknown."
> —Louis Horst, <u>Modern Dance Forms</u>

In choreography this process is called *theme* and *variation*. You start with a theme, and you work from that theme by making one or several variations that highlight different facets of the theme. In the end, you have a nice, long dance in which many interesting things have happened. We hope. But we can do better than hope by looking at some options for creating variations that will be a gift to watch.

Variations of movement themes can consist of

1. the statement of the theme, followed by a contrast: A B;
2. theme, variation, and repetition of original theme: A B A;
3. theme, contrasting variation, repetition of theme, a second contrasting variation, and theme again: A B A C A (This is called *rondo form*.); and
4. theme, variation, another variation, another, and so on: A A1 A2 A3.

You are still working with a theme as long as the elements of the theme remain in the same order (or sequence). Let us look at these variations one by one.

### AB Variation

This is the simplest form of all. AB variation is the on-the-other-hand form where you set up one theme and then present a contrast. Light and dark. Open and closed. Earth and sky. Love and hate.

With AB variation you generally use B to highlight some aspect of A, and that highlight provides the statement that the dance makes. The song "America the Beautiful" is an example of this kind of variation. The "Oh beautiful . . ." part is the A and "America, America, God shed His grace on Thee . . ." is the B variation, differing in melodic theme from the first half.

### ABA Variation

The children's song "Three Blind Mice" is a good example of ABA variation. The melody is established and repeated twice, then transposed up four notes and repeated twice more. Then the "they all ran after the farmer's wife" part provides a contrast to the original theme. This variation gets repeated three times, and the song concludes with a repetition of the A theme with the return of the words "three blind mice." Much popular music uses this kind of variation. The melody is introduced, followed by a bridge or a B melody, and the song returns to the A melody to conclude.

*theme and variation*

ABA is a very popular form that satisfies an instinctive sense of symmetry, a cycle that returns to its own beginning. This kind of symmetry can be reassuring, but it can also be boring if inappropriately applied. If tempted to conclude as you have begun, check to make sure that something has happened in the meantime!

Suppose you do not have a narrative or dramatic theme with which you want to work, but rather you have an abstract theme created from a string of movement words. Suppose your sequence is:

**Run     Turn     Drop     Leap**

Your dance might open with a combination of steps arranged in that sequence. Section A might be about all the ways that the dancers can run, turn, drop, and leap. Let us say that the music is bright, light, and sunny. Then comes section B, which offers a contrast to A. Let us say that the dancers still try to run, turn, drop, and leap, but the music to which this section is set is slow, somber, and somewhat dark. The music returns to the A theme and so does the choreography, although not exactly; there are glimpses of the slow, somber, or shadowy aspects that were revealed in section B. A: introduce, B: develop, A: recapitulate.

Here's another scenario. Your dance might open with lots of running followed by lots of turning, then lots of dropping, and, finally, you guessed it, lots of leaping. End of Section 1. Section 2 might feature a solo of all the ways you could run. Section 3 might feature another dancer who explores only turning. Thus, the recapitulation section calls into focus the importance of turning.

## ABACAD—Rondo Form

The rondo form is a very old musical form dating back at least to 15th-century music. In this form the theme is stated followed by some contrast or digression, after which the theme is restated, and yet another contrast or digression is offered. This process makes up the piece.

In dance things work the same way. Let us take the sequence above as our theme and suppose that the dancers begin with a sophisticated version of run, turn, drop, and leap, followed by a phrase that only includes running, and after which we see the run-turn-drop-leap sequence repeated. What might be a good contrast or digression around which to build the C variation?

## A-A1-A2-A3

The last sectional form in our list of strategies for variations is the add-in form in which the original theme is still perceptible but, with each new variation, the dance moves on never to return to the original form of the opening sequence. This is an evolutionary form. It is cumulative.

These forms are intended to be used as a guide for helping you structure your variations; they are not intended to be used as rigid molds into which you pour your dances. These forms are also useful to bear in mind when watching other people's choreography. Looking for the ways in which familiar material is introduced and re-introduced will give you a sense of what the choreographer feels is important in the dance.

## Development

> "A journey that begins with a question raised through disbelief, fueled by faith, navigated by instinct, and in search of the truth."
>
> —Nomad

Consider this story line: She was attracted to him, but he was involved with cars and did not know she was alive. He becomes attracted to her, but she has lost interest. Finally, they both like each other. They have an argument, and they both hate each other. They get back together. Love-hate, love-hate, love-hate. Then she is abducted by aliens from another galaxy; he realizes he liked racing cars better than girls anyway. The end.

Floppy, loose, lazy. Alert, upright, attentive. Quick, light, whimsical. Tired, strained, compulsive. Floppy, loose, exhausted. No story line. The end.

No story, but through using this development of qualities, a life experience is suggested without being detailed, allowing the audience to read this progression in their own way.

Finally, a valid answer to the question "What happens?" may well be: "Nothing." Should this be the choreographer's response, then even that nothingness will have its own significance. In the work of Merce Cunningham, for instance, one might observe that nothing happens; however, that presentation is consistent with his philosophy of concert dance. What happens in many nonliteral, modern or ballet performances may be equally hard to sum up.

---

Development will be guided by the methods of variation you use, but at the beginning stages there are some strategies for exploring different kinds of development that might help direct the work. Here are a few structures for development that you may find useful:

- Find a way to lose control at some point.
- Accelerate.
- Intensify in time, space, or effort.
- Create an inner monologue (that is, talk to yourself as you work).
- Talk to an invisible person as you work, describing what you are doing and why.
- Move continuously for a set period of time, 60 seconds to start with, and increase to 3 minutes. Do not allow yourself to settle on one spot at any time. Move continuously for a set period, and do not allow yourself to move from one spot at any time.

## Climax

*"An outcome that, though unforseen, was predicted from the start."*
                    —Robert Frost, <u>The Figure a Poem Makes</u>

The climax of a dance is basically the same as climax in a story, except that in a story a chronology of events culminates and in a dance an apex of energy is reached. If the dance tells a story then, most likely, some people have had some problem which comes to a head. If the dance does not tell a story, then their efforts most likely carry them to some point of no return. The music will often assist both the choreographer and the audience when determining this point of evolution. Sometimes there is a dramatic element that will let us know. Choreographic tools discussed in the section on variation give us further clues almost intuitively, as Horst suggests. If the theme has been well established, and the development is intelligible, the audience can often sense the return of the A, note the changes that have occurred, and sense the head toward home. Nonliteral dance climaxes are often accomplished by so embellishing the theme or so complicating the tasks of the dancers that the piece practically explodes. Other methods of creating more subtle explosions might be to establish constraints out of which the dance finally evolves, or establish constraints under which the dance finally collapses.

## Resolution

*"Begin at the beginning . . . and go on till you come to the end: then stop."*
                    —Lewis Carroll, <u>Alice's Adventures in Wonderland</u>

Doris Humphrey (1895-1958), one of the pioneers of modern dance, proscribed establishing a beginning *and an end* to one's dances before proceeding with the development. There is value in clarifying one's direction or focus at some point in the creative process. At our stage of choreographic investigation, however, I would recommend discovering the resolution to your work based on your experience in the piece using feedback from the three modes of perception.

➡ What do you want your final image to look like? Fleeting? Dying? Resting? Invigorated? Elated? Contorted?

➡ What do you want your final image to sound like? Heavy? Weightless? Shifty? Slippery?

➡ What do you feel, and what kinesthetic effect would you like your audience to have, in resolution of your efforts? Nervous? Thrilled? Pained? At ease?

These seven principles must not be confused with a flowchart of creation. In real life, each is considered and reconsidered as the work assumes a life of its own. When establishing contrast, you may discover that repetition needs to be more obvious or more subtle. Thoughtful attention to transition may take you into a new variation, and suddenly the development you had so neatly anticipated is no longer relevant! Your climax may come as you speed up or as you slow down. Your climax and resolution may be simultaneous. You may not have a resolution. These are elements that will *probably* exist in a piece with a clear focus and that makes a moving (though not necessarily explicable) impact on the audience. These principles may be a useful resource to you if you suspect that your work is not quite accomplishing what you had hoped. Consider them references more than doctrines.

## How to Make a Dance

Would it be nice if the directions for dance-making were simple enough to condense into a little booklet so that if you wanted to make a dance, all you had to do was flip through, follow the instructions, and voilà! Well, maybe it would not be so great after all. Maybe all dances would look the same or so similar that if you have seen one dance, you have seen them all. Maybe it is just as well that composing a dance still requires a lot of experimentation, discovering, and trial and error. And maybe it is just as well that not everyone agrees on what makes a good dance and what makes a not-so-good dance. Tastes, styles, and designs of any art evolve to suit the needs of the culture they serve. Dance tastes, styles, and designs hopefully evolve along with the culture they serve.

Dance composition is an on-going process. Even supposedly finished work often changes as new dancers learn old roles, a dance needs to be adapted to a new space, or a slight variation is suggested that might improve the work. In fact, it has been suggested that one can never see the same dance twice. There is a magic that is created with every performance, and no one can guarantee what kind of magic that will be until the dance is over.

Composition—whether dance, literature, music, sculpture, or, yes, even engine rebuilding—has moments of magic for the creator, moments when a piece of the puzzle suddenly fits. The frequency of these moments depends on all of the things we have considered in this chapter: the primary considerations of function, materials, and audience—Why? How? For whom?; the investment of the composer, and the composer's willingness to do the exploratory work necessary to go beyond simply rearranging what has already been done, to take the risk of making a personal leap of faith into composing; the ability to respond to the world and to integrate new information so that the perspective offered by the composition is a creative unity; and the use of the principles of composition as a guide for expanding the work so that it goes beyond being simply personal and is a gift that makes sense.

How to make a dance? Begin!

## Think About It

1. What is the function of the opening number that the contestants at the Miss America Pageant learn and perform? If you were hired to create that dance, how would you consider function, materials, and audience when composing this opening dance?

2. Marcel Duchamps was an artist who submitted a urinal to a museum as a piece of sculpture. It was displayed as sculpture, not as a functioning toilet. An artist in New York City put a picture frame around some exposed pipes in her apartment and signed the wall in the right hand corner of the framed area. In these cases, how do function, materials, and audience relate to composition? Do you think these artists can be credited with composition? If a dancer takes steps he has learned in class, and uses those steps in a dance, has he composed a dance?

3. How are function, materials, and audience part of your work in class? That is, would you handle an assignment differently if you were going to show your work to a church group? Or the entire student body? Or a local-TV news reporter? Or a close friend? How are you influenced by the fact that your work is graded rather than merely applauded?

4. How would you describe the difference between a composition and an arrangement? Do you think the creative process involved with each one is different? How important is tradition to either process? Under what circumstances would one approach be preferable to the other? Which do you find easier for yourself as a creative process? How would you distinguish between composition and arrangement in music? In writing reports?

5. A composer is responsible for integrating life experience through composition. Think of one experience you had today that could be developed into a dance composition. Think of one experience you had today that could be developed into a composition in another medium (music, sculpture, literature, or video).

6. Is form preferable to chaos? How? Why?

7. How do the principles of composition apply to the writing of a lab report? How might these principles be applied to make a repetitive job more interesting? How might these principles be applied to a friendship or a relationship?

# 12

# Is This a Good Dance?

**E**ager to expose students to the wonderful world of modern dance, a dance teacher arranged to have several first-year students attend a concert of a well-known New York dance company appearing in a nearby town. The lights dimmed and the first piece began. It was an abstract work with no specific plot or message. The set was nonexistent, and the dancers wore plain dark leotards. The dancers were leaping and balancing, apparently according to plan, but about 15 minutes into the piece, one of the students tapped the teacher on the shoulder and whispered cautiously, "Excuse me, but is this a good dance?"

Have you ever found yourself wondering the same thing as you watch the work of your peers or the work of professional dancers (Figure 12.1)? Have you ever wondered how to judge the merit of your creative endeavors? This chapter will give you the tools needed to help you identify the goals of a dance so that you will be in a better position to evaluate the success of the work in a constructive and supportive framework. In other chapters we have discussed similarities between the creative process in dance and other creative activities. In the same way, the evaluation process we will pursue here will also be useful for developing skills for evaluating other creative activities.

## The Creative Act

The creative act is motivated from many different sources. Some create to satisfy their own curiosity, to gain notoriety, to solve problems, or to prompt questions. Whatever the source, there is ultimately an idea or a product that is an offering to the world—

171

### Figure 12.1

The Nutcracker has been produced millions of times by both amateur and professional companies. Different audiences choose different performances for different reasons.

an idea or product which is that person's best effort at synthesizing experiences, perceptions, sensations, and personal wisdom, all formed to be shared as a gift. A 10-year-old's piano rendition of "*Frere Jacques*" is as much a gift to the world as the PhD's cancer research paper. A beginning dance student's 60-second dance study is as much a gift to the world as the evening-length work of an internationally renowned choreographer. Whether evaluating your own efforts or the efforts of others, it is important to bear in mind that the creative effort is an offering that has value to its creator.

## Evaluating Your Own Work

If you are evaluating your work, you will want to consider all the ways that the work you have created has value for you. What gift have you made to yourself in this creative process? When answering this question, consider the physical, social, and emotional aspects of personal growth.

- ➡ Through this creative process have you discovered new physical capabilities?
- ➡ Through this creative process have you any new insights about yourself as a social being? New insights about other people? New insights about the way the world works?

➥ Through this creative process have you grown emotionally? Have you stretched yourself through risk-taking? Have you persevered through frustration?

➥ Through this creative process what gift have you made to the world? Is your personal development gift enough, or do you have another agenda for being an effective and vital part of the planet?

## Evaluating the Work of Others

If you are evaluating the work of others, you will want to be clear about the purpose of your evaluation. In other words, for whose benefit is your evaluation? Are you describing the work for the benefit of someone who missed the performance? Are you placing the work in a social or historical context for someone who did not understand it? Are you attempting to provide helpful feedback for the choreographer? Are you using the work as a soapbox to discuss your own ideas or aesthetics?

When evaluating someone else's work, you are going through a process of critical thinking that enables you to determine the value of that work in a particular context. If your goal is to place the work in the context of your life experience, then it is appropriate to respond personally and to consider the ways in which you were affected by the piece, the things you liked or did not like, you would have done differently, you admired, and so on. This kind of evaluation is self-serving.

Another kind of evaluation is that which serves the creator of the work. If your goal is to help the creator determine the value of the work, then your own agenda is less relevant (if relevant at all). Your task is to help the creator by entertaining specific questions about the work and by asking neutral, nonjudgmental questions of the artist. This process works best if the creator has specific questions to which you, the critic, can respond. Questions like, "Did you think it was too boring?" invite the critic to judge the piece rather than assist in its evaluation. A better question might be, "Was there too much repetition in the first section?" This invites a discussion of the value of the repetition rather than the criteria of one person's definition of what is boring.

A third kind of evaluation is that which assesses the value of the work in social or historical contexts. A reporter does this when describing the work for a public who did not attend. A description of the work accompanies an informal or formal judgment that supposedly enables the readers to assume the value this piece would have had in their lives had they been present.

There are three focuses in an evaluation:

1. Evaluation can be self-serving, enabling the critic to find the value of the work in the context of that critic's life.

2. Evaluation can be creator-serving, where the critic's function is to assist the creator in determining what aspects of the piece have value for the creator.

3. Evaluation can be public-serving, enabling the public—those who did not witness the actual performance—to suppose what value the piece would have had in their lives had they been present.

People are awkward and hesitant about both giving and getting criticism because it is easy to hurt feelings. When people offer criticism, you can expect that they will start off with some complimentary comments, followed by some not-so-complimentary comments, and concluded with some words of encouragement. This flow is meant to put you in a positive frame of mind so you will feel that your self-worth is not being threatened and that you will be receptive to a few gently worded comments about the ways in which your work was not perfect. Although this formula can sound predictable, it does, at least, guarantee that the person who is invested in the piece receives immediate praise for the work.

## Words of Criticism

We have tossed around several different words that all belong in the realm of criticism without really clarifying some of their different applications. Let us look at the language of criticism. Begin with the critic. Giving criticism has come to mean describing all that is wrong with something, but that is not using the word with complete accuracy. The root of "criticism" obviously comes from "critic," derived from the Greek *kritikos*, meaning "able to discern or judge." The critic is someone who expresses a reasoned opinion on any matter involving a judgment of value, truth, or righteousness; the opinion may also be an appreciation of the work's beauty, technique, or interpretation.

Value. Truth. Righteousness. Beauty. Those are some fairly broad concepts on which to offer a reasoned opinion. Who *is* entitled to offer such opinions? Are you? Are your friends? Are your classmates? Are your teachers? And who gets to decide what is a reasoned opinion?

We have also used the word "evaluate" in place of criticize. How would you say these two words differ?

"Consider" is another word we have used in almost the same way as "criticize." What is the difference for you among these three words? Are they interchangeable? Do they each imply a different commitment to the judgment being offered? Do they each imply a different breadth of experience? Do they each imply a different level of objectivity?

What about objective and subjective? Are you clear on the difference between them? Objective assessments are based on impersonal observation, as in, "The costume was green, yellow, and orange." When people claim to be making objective criticism, they are claiming to be observing impartially without the interference of personal taste or judgment. Subjective assessments are based on personal experience or feelings, as in, "I think the costume is ugly." These two perspectives can easily become muddled in the arena of criticism.

Other words that often come up in critical discussions are words that have vastly different meanings for different people and are, therefore, dangerous to interject unless you know that your value system and aesthetics are the same as those of your audience. Consider beauty. What are *your* criteria for beauty? To some, a trimmed-out Harley Davidson is a thing of beauty; to others it is just a motorcycle. To some, purple-dyed, spiked hair is a beautiful style; to others it is an aberration.

Context is another all-important word. The way you choose to address your criticism (as self-serving, artist-serving, or public-serving) will indicate the context of your remarks. Honest, self-serving criticism will include a lot of ownership of the opinions, as in, "I thought it looked like a swamp of alligators," or "I found it hard to look at the color red for so long." These personal statements remind the listener that the criticism being expressed relates directly and subjectively to the life and experience of the speaker or critic. With self-serving criticism, the speaker is really only obliged to share personal experience of the work and is not obliged to second-guess the intentions of the choreographer or the relation of the work to other dances.

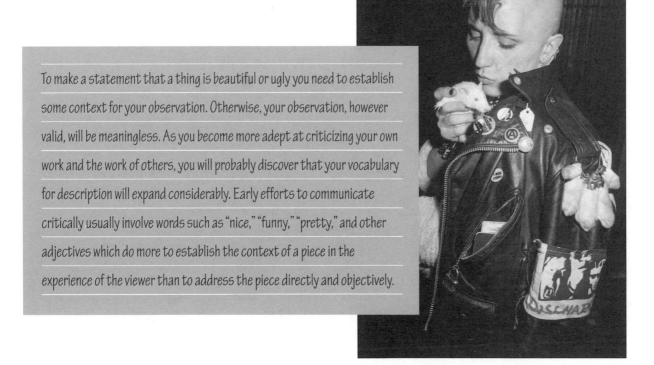

To make a statement that a thing is beautiful or ugly you need to establish some context for your observation. Otherwise, your observation, however valid, will be meaningless. As you become more adept at criticizing your own work and the work of others, you will probably discover that your vocabulary for description will expand considerably. Early efforts to communicate critically usually involve words such as "nice," "funny," "pretty," and other adjectives which do more to establish the context of a piece in the experience of the viewer than to address the piece directly and objectively.

Criticism made in the context of serving the artist obliges the critic to consider the intentions of the artist and personally respond to the effectiveness with which those intentions were revealed. As we shall discuss below, if the artist does not invite these responses or cannot be clear about the intentions of the piece, then the criticism ceases to be artist-serving and reverts to being self-serving.

Criticism made in the context of serving the public is the most suspicious of all; the critic's personal preferences are quite likely to be woven into the evaluation, but they may be presented as fact rather than opinion. To be sure, there are many who are able to be objective, place their remarks in the frame of history, and accurately describe a piece so that those who missed the performance would have a sense of what they had missed. Critics who are good at composing this kind of evaluation are able to create a context in which the value of a piece can be assessed.

## Recognizing, Interpreting, and Creating Relevance

If your evaluation is self-serving, then your evaluation will focus on the value the dance had in the context of your life and experiences. The process of determining this value is a process of recognizing, interpreting, or creating some relevance between your experiences and the dance you have seen. It is not necessary that you correctly guess the intentions of the choreographer in order to recognize, interpret, or create some relevance in your life. It is only necessary that you are willing to find a way to consider the images and ideas to which you have been exposed in the context of your life.

For instance, let us suppose that you have attended a performance of *The Nutcracker*. Let us further suppose that the reason you attended is not out of some deep love for the music or the ballet itself but, rather, to support the efforts of a friend who was in the performance. The value you find in this dance experience may have less to do with the aesthetics of ballet and more to do with admiring your graceful friend. Finding a value for the dance in the context of your life and experiences, you might be drawn to reflect on your friend's attraction to dance or level of physical fitness relative to your own. It may be that what impresses you most about the production is not the dancing itself but is, instead, the elaborate sets and costumes. What value could such spectacle have in your life? If, however, your evaluation is not self-serving, that is, if you are offering an evaluation in order to assist the creator, or if you are offering an evaluation in order to report on the work for the benefit of others, then it is necessary that you consider the intention of the choreographer. You can assume that the choreographer has contemplated what the function of the piece should be, what materials would be best to work with, and what the target audience would be (Figure 12.2).

### Function

Some questions to consider relative to function include:

➡ What was the driving force that created this piece?

➡ What was the vision being pursued?

**Figure 12.2**
A well-constructed dance will leave the audience with images that resonate weeks after the performance.

➥ What was the primary purpose? To instruct? To explore? To expose? To inspire? To entertain?

Let us look at evaluating function in your own work and in the work of others.

In the process of creating a piece one does not necessarily know what the function of the piece will be. In fact, as we discussed in the chapter on composition, it is quite likely that the original impetus will be substantially modified by the time you have finished your improvisational research.

Let us suppose you have been given an assignment to choreograph a study based on the contrast between open and closed. In this case, the driving force to create the piece is grade-motivated. However, in the course of experimenting with open and closed shapes and movements you discover that what interests you is your personal discovery that closed shapes and movements make you feel safe, and open shapes and movements make you feel vulnerable. As you continue to explore being safe and being vulnerable, the driving force changes from just wanting to get a good grade to wanting to understand and to express something that has meaning for you. You now have a vision, and the piece has a purpose.

By the time it is necessary to polish the work, it should be possible for you, the creator, to assess what has been made and to direct the work toward a function that is coherent. After all, when you ultimately present your work you are asking your audience to find a context for your ideas in their own lives, so it does behoove you to at least have a point of view.

Ideally, when you present your work you should be able to articulate the function the piece has for you. The value of this piece—the function of this work in your life—may particularly pertain to physical, emotional, or social interests you wish to explore.

When you can be clear about the function you wish your piece to serve, you can be equally clear about the kind of criticism that you are most interested in receiving from your critics. If the function of your piece was to stretch yourself technically by trying to work at a speed that was uncommon for you, you might be interested in hearing from people who could put this latest work in perspective with your earlier work to see whether or not you were successful. You might be interested in knowing if your audience found your movement choices interesting, attractive, compelling, or otherwise worth watching.

If the function of your piece was to arouse empathy, you might be curious to know whether anyone was moved emotionally by your work. Having specific questions will help your critics respond with information that is useful to you. For example, asking, "Did you like it?" will probably not generate feedback that will be specific enough to help you to make improvements. However, asking, "What images were particularly strong?" or "What adjectives or adverbs would you use to describe the piece?" will give you responses that help you to gauge how well the work served the function you intended.

If the function of your piece was to educate or testify, you might not care at all about people's comments on the technical aspects of the work; you might only be interested in whether they were persuaded to adopt your point of view.

When evaluating your own work, start by examining the function of the work. Look at both the product and the process. "Is this a good dance?" is a question you will have answered when you have found the value that dance has in your life.

If you are evaluating the function of someone else's work, you will need to be aware of who is being served by your evaluation. If the evaluation is for your own benefit, it will be up to you to find a function that the piece can serve in your experience. Sometimes this is easy; sometimes this takes generous thought.

## Materials

We have said in the previous chapter that the materials for a dance will come from the choreographer's experiences. When criticizing a dance—your own or someone else's—you need to consider what experiences this person might or might not have to offer.

Beginning composition students can often be extraordinarily inventive because their (usually limited) exposure to dance leaves them little to compare with their own work. They often solve problems in a simple, direct, and unpretentious way because they are not trying to duplicate someone else's work. The person criticizing a beginning composition, therefore, needs to maintain the perspective of a beginning student and find value in the freshness of the composition and the skill of this person's early attempts to work with the principles of composition.

Without apologizing, both creator and critic need to keep in mind the materials that have been chosen for the work. What is the scope of the work? Is it within the capacity of the choreographer to address this scope? What technical requirements have been placed on the dancers? Are these requirements within their capacities? What choices have been made pertaining to supporting structures, such as music, text, props, costumes, and lighting? Are these choices ones which serve the goals of the piece, or does the piece serve these structures?

The same questions will be applicable to the criticism of the work of a more mature choreographer, but one would expect the standards to be a little more sophisticated and rigorous. When considering scope, for instance, a beginning student might be faulted for adopting too broad a theme while an advanced student might be encouraged to tackle an issue more fully and deeply. And technically, it would be assumed that a more advanced dancer and choreographer would make more specific demands on the dancers, not necessarily in terms of human tricks, but requiring completed lines, pointed feet, extended limbs, and so on. It would also be assumed that the choreography would have its own integrity supported by, but not reliant upon, the supporting structures.

## Audience

The intention of the piece must finally be considered in terms of the audience for which it was designed. Just as it would be unfair to chastise a 5-year-old for not recognizing the value of a fine piece of crystal, so it would be inappropriate to expect that audiences new to dance will have the experiences they need to find a context for abstract work. When creating, you need to make decisions about what your target audience is going to be in order to offer a gift that will make sense to them. It is not different from buying a sweater for a gift. You consider what is going to fit, what colors are going to be appreciated, and what climate the receiver inhabits as you narrow your choices. It is not different from choosing your words carefully and deliberately when trying to express yourself in a foreign language. You want to be understood, so you put some effort into speaking in intelligible terms.

When considering the audience, function and material considerations still play a part. For instance, if you are preparing a study knowing that the audience will be your composition class, you might be less inclined to throw in some sure-fire crowd pleasers than you might be if you were preparing a study that would be an audition piece. Consider what risks are important for you to be taking and what circumstances you would consider safe for such risk-taking.

When evaluating someone else's work, consider what audience the work was intended to serve. The general public? Young audiences? Audiences familiar to dance? Audiences looking forward to a challenge? Audiences looking forward to being reassured by something familiar?

## What Does This Dance Have to Do With Me?

How are you supposed to evaluate something that you did not understand? The process of evaluating dance, or any creative endeavor, is in itself a creative act. Whether you are evaluating your own work or someone else's work, you are really asking yourself the question, "What does this have to do with me?"

Particularly in the context of a composition class, you will be called upon to respond to the work of your peers. This kind of evaluation requires generosity, creativity, and often a good bit of tact because you will want to preserve good relations while maintaining your own integrity. Your goal should be to create a critical dialogue that is nonthreatening and positive. Here are some examples of affirmative, nonthreatening responses:

1.  Use adjectives creatively and honestly: "I thought the piece was very . . . . " (powerful, graceful, touching, humorous, clever, provocative, disturbing, etc.)

2.  Comment about the execution: "It was well rehearsed." "You made good use of the skills of the performers." "You used the space in an interesting manner."

3.  Comment about the development of the artist as evidenced by the work: "You are using more contrast and variety in this work that in previous pieces." "The repetition of the phrase was very effective."

4.  Ask the artist for explanations instead of voicing your opinion: Rather than saying, "Why did you use those stupid shoes?" try, "I was surprised by the choice of shoes. Can you talk about that choice?" Rather than saying, "It didn't make any sense to me when you kept going back to the wall," try, "Can you talk about the repetition of the return to the wall?"

Your responsibilities as a critic are twofold: (1) not to bring your own agenda to the work you are responding to and (2) to have a desire for the artist to do the artist's best work. You should attempt to help the artist create a piece, not to create your own. It is important for you, as hard as this may be, not to bring your biases and expectations to the process.

## The Third Hat: A Reporter's Evaluation

When you do not have the benefit of conferring with the artist and you feel obliged to evaluate, as a reporter would, for the benefit of someone who did not witness the performance, what guidelines are appropriate?

First, take notice of your audience. That is, as much as possible, try to place the work in the context of other, related dance works so that the value of the piece you are describing has relevance to the experience of your audience independent of your experience.

Second, make your subjective assessments (opinions) clearly identifiable and distinguishable from general wisdom. Rather than implying that everyone in the audience found a piece to be boring, stimulating, dull, or challenging, make it clear that these are *your* opinions.

Third, try to be as objectively descriptive as possible. The dancer wore red. The men wore the same costumes—which happened to be dresses—as the women. The music was contemporary, atonal, melodic, whatever. This kind of description again allows the person who is listening to determine the supposed value of the piece in the context of that person's life rather than the context of your life.

Finally, use the elements of dance and the principles of composition as a structure and framework for your comments.

## Is This a Good Dance?

Ultimately, you are the best and only true judge of a work of art because you alone will be able or unable to find value in it. As promised at the beginning of this chapter, the guidelines discussed can be applied to evaluating any creative endeavor. The guidelines can be applied to work that is your own or someone else's.

A dance is good if it has relevance to your life. This relevance may be immediately obvious or it may take some effort to discover. The next section contains questions that may help you to consider and to discover the value of a work of art.

### Some Considerations for Critical Feedback

The following questions were developed by Linda Burnham, Founder of High Performance Magazine, Co-Director of Art in the Public Interest, Saxapahaw, NC (first presented at an annual meeting of Alternate ROOTS, Black Mountain, NC).

1. What was the piece about?
2. Who is it coming from—out of what community?
3. What is the artist trying to do? Teach? Tell a story? Create a feeling? Change your mind? Change your vision?
4. At what point in the piece did you realize that? Should that have come earlier?
5. How did the structure of the piece reveal itself to you?
6. Was the form suitable to the content?
7. What part did language, visual elements, sound elements play in the piece, and how did it (they) communicate?
8. Was the artist in control of the medium?
9. Did the artist *push* the subject matter or rely on available stereotypes and media clichés?
10. Was the piece lazy? Obvious?
11. Where did the artist go in deep and take a chance?
12. Did the artist try to take clichés and stereotypes and turn them inside out?

13. Whose experience informs this piece—the artist's own?

14. Did the artist attempt to make art outside of the artist's culture?

15. Did the artist show us workable ways to draw on the experience of others?

16. What cultural symbols were used, and how were they treated—thoughtfully or casually?

17. Were they loaded symbols—highly significant to one or more cultures?

18. Did you learn something about the world that you did not know before?

19. Did the piece take a global view? Did it contribute to the picture of our multicultural society?

20. Did it show us how we can share each other's experience without losing individual identities and making a bland mush of the culture? How?

21. Was the artist guilty of cultural piracy? How?

22. If you go away from this piece with just one image, what will it be and how will you feel about holding it?

23. On a scale of 1 to 10, did you like it?

## Think About It

1. Do you think it is possible to create dances in which you have no investment, that is, dances which offer no physical, emotional, or social challenges to you? What value could these dances have for you?

2. What brand of criticism is most comfortable for you to give: self-serving, artist-serving, or public-serving? What brand of criticism is most comfortable for you to receive?

3. By what criteria do you measure your success as a creative person?

# Acknowledgments

I find that Western culture perceives artists as people out of the mainstream. At the very least, it calls those who find joy in creating works of art "special"; more often society labels them as "eccentric," "weird," or (gratuitously) "unique." The Puritan-influenced mind has trouble fathoming the value of physical celebration or the delight of spontaneity. The dollar-oriented mind has difficulty making a logical cost analysis of the time spent vs. profit accrued. Clearly, it does not "make sense" to create art if these parameters define the worth of such pursuits. In this climate, artists need strong support systems in order to feel that their ideas, visions, and creations do indeed have value. Many creative people do have the strength to sing their own songs, write their own poems, paint their own paintings, and choreograph their own dances without depending on others for validation. I am not one of those people. I am one of the lucky ones who has crossed or shared paths with people who have helped me sustain my vision and grow as a dancer, choreographer, writer, and woman.

I am deeply indebted to my husband, Clay Rowan, who has been a generous and critical reader and a stalwart supporter. My parents, Gustav and Betsy Schrader, have given me the confidence to write and the moral incentive to complete this project. Professor Jim McGlinn's feedback and encouragement in the early stages were tremendously important. Likewise, Professor Pamela Sofras, a resource to thousands of dance educators, cheered me on when I doubted my vision. On the road to discovering who I am and what I have to offer the world, I am grateful to have been joined by Carolyn Rosenthal, a remarkably vital woman who lives by the motto: "Be patient, God's not finished with me yet." And speaking of remarkable women, Peggy Lawler, my mentor and friend, influenced my sense of dance 20 years ago. And thank you Rob Pulleyn, arbiter of style, for your stamp of approval.

Other friends—Julie Gillum, Barrie Barton, Mary Ann Osby, and Ali Bush—helped me test a lot of this material in their public school classes and gave me valuable feedback. I also thank Larret Galasyn-Wright, the developmental editor who tackled and tamed this beast of a book. Finally, I extend thanks to the thousands of students over the years who have helped me learn to teach by being willing to learn.

# Index